A Reading Skills Book

interactions one

A Reading Skills Book

Third Edition

interactions one

Elaine Kirn
West Los Angeles College

Pamela Hartmann
Los Angeles Unified School District

The McGraw-Hill Companies, Inc.
New York   St. Louis   San Francisco   Auckland   Bogotá   Caracas
Lisbon   London   Madrid   Mexico City   Milan   Montreal   New Delhi
San Juan   Singapore   Sydney   Tokyo   Toronto

This is an book.

McGraw-Hill

A Division of The McGraw-Hill Companies

Interactions One
A Reading Skills Book
Third Edition

6 7 8 9 0   DOC DOC   9 0 9 8

ISBN 0-07-034917-7
ISBN 0-07-114370-X

This book was set in Times Roman by Monotype Composition Company, Inc. The editors were
Tim Stookesberry, Bill Preston, and Karen Davy; the designers were Lorna Lo, Suzanne Mon-
tazer, Francis Owens, and Elizabeth Williamson; the production supervisor was Patricia Myers;
the cover was designed by Francis Owens; the cover illustrator was Susan Pizzo; the photo re-
searcher was Cindy Robinson, Seaside Publishing; illustrations were done by David Bohn, Rick
Hackney, and Lori Heckelman.

R. R. Donnelley & Sons Company, Crawfordsville, IN, was printer and binder.
Phoenix Color Corporation was cover separator and printer.

Library of Congress Catalog Card Number: 95-80831

INTERNATIONAL EDITION
Copyright 1996. Exclusive rights by The McGraw-Hill Companies, Inc. for manufacture and
export. This book cannot be re-exported from the country to which it is consigned by McGraw-
Hill. The International Edition is not available in North America.

When ordering this title, use ISBN 0-07-114370-X.

This book is printed on acid-free paper.

Photo credits: *Page 1* © Aronson Photographics/Stock, Boston; *21* © Jeff Greenberg/Photo-
Edit; *28* © Ray S. Conklin/PhotoEdit; *39* © Walter Gilardetti; *59* © John Fung; *71* © R.
Michael Stuckey/Comstock; *75, 77* © John Fung; *79 (top)* © W. B. Spunbarg/PhotoEdit; *(bottom)* © Tom Prettyman/PhotoEdit; *81* © Myrleen Ferguson Cate/PhotoEdit, *97 (top)* © Tara C.
Patty/Jeroboam Inc.; *(bottom)* © Robert Brenner/PhotoEdit; *101* © Phil McCarten/PhotoEdit;
117 © Michael Newman/PhotoEdit; *125* © John Fung; *127* © H. Confer/The Image Works;
137 © Stacy Pick/Stock, Boston, *153* © Robert Brenner/PhotoEdit, *175* © Daryl Goldberg;
197 © Barbara Rios/Photo Researchers, Inc.; *219* © Walter Gilardetti; *225* © Aronson
Photographics/Stock, Boston; *227* © Tom McCarthy/PhotoEdit; *230* © Gary Wagner/Stock,
Boston; *241* © Walter Gilardetti

Contents

CHAPTER **one**

School Life   *1*

CHAPTER **two**

Experiencing Nature   *21*

CHAPTER **three**

Living to Eat or Eating to Live?   *39*

CHAPTER seven

Health   127

CHAPTER eight

Entertainment and the Media   153

CHAPTER nine

Social Life   175

The Interactions One Program

The Interactions One program consists of five texts and a variety of supplemental materials for high-beginning to low-intermediate students seeking to improve their English language skills. Each of the five texts in this program is carefully organized by chapter theme, vocabulary, grammar structures, and, where possible, language functions. As a result, information introduced in a chapter of any one of the Interactions One texts corresponds to and reinforces material taught in the same chapter of the other four books, creating a truly integrated, four-skills approach.

The Interactions One program is highly flexible. The texts in this series may be used together or separately, depending on students' needs and course goals. The books in this program include:

- **A Communicative Grammar Book.** Organized around grammatical topics, this book includes notional/functional material where appropriate. It presents all grammar in context and contains many types of communicative activities.
- **A Listening / Speaking Skills Book.** This book uses lively, natural language from various contexts, including dialogues, interviews, lectures, and announcements. Listening strategies emphasized include summarizing main ideas, making inferences, listening for stressed words, reductions, and intonation. A variety of speaking activities complement the listening components.
- **A Reading Skills Book.** The reading selections contain sophisticated college-level material; however, vocabulary and grammar have been carefully controlled to be at students' level of comprehension. The text includes many vocabulary-building exercises and emphasizes reading strategies such as skimming, scanning, guessing meaning from context, understanding the structure and organization of a selection, increasing reading speed, and interpreting the author's point of view.
- **A Writing Process Book.** This book uses a process approach to writing, including many exercises on prewriting and revision. Exercises build skills in exploring and organizing ideas; developing vocabulary; using correct form and mechanics; using coherent structure; and editing, revising, and using feedback to create a final draft.
- **A Multi-Skills Activity Book.** New to this edition, this text gives students integrated practice in all four language skills. Among the communicative activities included in this text are exercises for the new video program that accompanies the Interactions One series.

Supplemental Materials

In addition to the five core texts outlined above, various supplemental materials are available to assist users of the third edition, including:

Instructor's Manual

Extensively revised for the new edition, this manual provides instructions and guidelines for using the five core texts separately or in various combinations to suit particular program needs. For each of the core texts, there is a separate section with teaching tips, additional activities, and other suggestions. The testing materials have been greatly expanded in this edition.

Audio Program for Interactions One: A Listening/Speaking Skills Book

Completely rerecorded for the new edition, the audio program is designed to be used in conjunction with those exercises that are indicated with a cassette icon in the student text. Complete tapescripts for all exercises are now included in the back of the student text.

Audio Program to Accompany Interactions One: A Reading Skills Book

This new optional audio program contains selected readings from the student text. These tape selections of poems, articles, stories, and speeches enable students to listen at their leisure to the natural oral discourse of native readers for imitation and modeling. Readings that are included in this program are indicated with a cassette icon in the student text.

Video

New to this edition, the video program for Interactions One contains authentic television segments that are coordinated with the twelve chapter themes in the five texts. Exercises and activities for this video are in the Multi-Skills Activities Book.

Interactions One: A Reading Skills Book, Third Edition

Rationale

Interactions One: A Reading Skills Book, third edition, is based on the idea that people learn to read by reading. If the material is interesting and not too difficult, students will enjoy reading and will be encouraged to read more; the more they read, the better they will be at it. The problem for academic ESL students is that they want to read more sophisticated material but lack the skills with which to do so.

The solution is twofold: (1) give students readings that are intellectually stimulating but not beyond their lexical, grammatical, or syntactic understanding; and (2) teach strategies that make reading easier. The reading selections in this book contain sophisticated material. However, vocabulary and grammar have been carefully controlled to be at the students' level of comprehension. In addition, the exercises guide students toward acquiring the skills of good readers, skills that make reading both easy and fun.

Vocabulary items presented in one chapter are recycled in subsequent chapters to prevent students from forgetting them. This constant recycling enables students to make rapid progress; their vocabulary will increase dramatically as they use the book, and yet this process will not be perceived as difficult.

One of the biggest obstacles to comprehension in many academic ESL reading texts is that the grammar is too difficult for high-beginning to low-intermediate students. In the reading selections of this book, however, the grammar points have been carefully sequenced and contextualized. This text is not only coordinated with the grammar text of the Interactions One program but is also compatible with the grammar sequencing found in most other high-beginning to low-intermediate ESL texts.

Note that because this is a reading text, grammar is not taught for the sake of grammar. Instead, it is seen as an aid to comprehension. Other such aids — or strategies — taught in this text include guessing meaning from context, increasing reading speed, understanding stems and affixes, making predictions, learning to accept some amount of uncertainty, and making inferences.

Although the material in this book may look difficult to students, they will find that the tasks they are required to perform with the material are not difficult. As a result, students will move through the book with a growing sense of confidence and accomplishment as they discover that they can find the main ideas, identify important details, and understand much of the new vocabulary without a dictionary. Moreover, academic students will feel intellectually challenged by material that engages their intelligence.

Chapter Organization

Because its primary purpose is to provide instruction in the reading process, this book offers numerous exercises and activities directed toward that end. It is left to individual teachers to choose those sections suited to the specific needs of their students. Each of the twelve chapters is divided into five parts as follows:

- **Part One** consists of brief prereading exercises, a reading selection (usually nonfiction), and postreading exercises that focus on four important reading skills: getting the main ideas, guessing the meaning from context, recognizing reading structure, and understanding details. These are followed by discussion questions that relate the reading selection to the student's own lives.
- **Part Two** contains a second reading selection (usually lighter than the first); exercises on skimming for main ideas, summarizing, recognizing the writer's point of view (Chapters Seven, Eight, and Twelve) and inferring meaning (Chapters Eight to Twelve); and more personalized discussion questions about the selection.
- **Part Three** contains various exercises to help students expand their passive and active vocabulary and acquire essential skills for academic reading, such as dictionary usage. New **Focus on Testing** exercises offer practice in study skills (such as identifying parts of speech, synonyms, antonyms, compound nouns) to help students prepare for standardized vocabulary tests.
- **Part Four** is a section of "realia" — food and medicine labels, advertisements, a page from a college catalog, and others — accompanied by

a short glossary and/or questions for students to use in scanning for specific information.
- **Part Five** includes one or more "personal stories" — brief, fictional, cross-cultural accounts of life in North America related to the chapter theme.

Teaching Suggestions

The following suggestions are designed to help teach the reading skills good readers use, skills essential to students' academic success.

Part One

Before You Read

The skill of anticipation — forming predictions about what is to be read — is an important part of active reading. To encourage this prereading skill, have students discuss the picture, answering the questions in the Getting Started section. Then read through the Preparing to Read questions. Tell students that they are not expected to be able to answer these questions before reading; instead, they should keep them in mind *as* they read. Since teachers disagree about the value of vocabulary preparation before reading, the Glancing at Vocabulary section is optional. Students can repeat each item after the teacher, for pronunciation practice, and learn the meaning later, or the teacher might introduce the meaning at this point, before the reading selection

Reading Selection

Each student should read the selection silently, which is the most common form of academic reading. The selection should be read quickly, without a dictionary. Encourage students to guess the meanings of new words. Emphasize the importance of getting the main idea — the most basic of reading skills.

If you prefer to have students listen to the reading selection as they read silently in order to reinforce listening comprehension, you might either read it aloud yourself or use the cassette tape that accompanies the book. (Do not have students read aloud because doing so interferes with both comprehension and speed.)

After You Read

A variety of exercises follow the reading selection; they are intended to help students acquire in English the same skills that good readers already have naturally in their native language. Emphasis is on getting the main ideas, guessing the meaning from context, recognizing reading structure, and understanding details. Have students complete the Getting the Main Ideas section, which checks comprehension of general themes and important ideas in the reading. Students should complete these ideas quickly, without looking back at the reading selection. The answers can be checked later, after students have reread the section.

The Guessing Meaning from Context section contains specific hints and step-by-step exercises about *how* to guess meanings of new words, thereby avoiding tedious and time-consuming trips to the dictionary. Many students lack the confidence to trust their own guess, and they tend to cling to a dictionary. They need to be told — probably repeatedly throughout the term — that it is not usually necessary to know *exactly* what a new word means or to know *everything* about it the first time they encounter it.

Have students reread the selection, this time more carefully, focusing on details. They might occasionally use a dictionary for this, although they still should be encouraged to apply the skills they have learned in the Guessing Meaning from Context section. When students finish rereading the selection, they should check their answers in the Getting the Main Ideas section before completing the other postreading exercises.

Students can actively practice their newly learned vocabulary words as they express their opinions and share ideas in the Discussing the Reading section. There are a number of ways to handle these discussion questions, including:

1. **Ask the questions of the entire class.** The advantage to this technique is that the teacher can control the discussion and encourage students to expand their ideas. The disadvantage, however, is that few students may volunteer to speak in a large group.
2. **Have students discuss the answers in small groups.** A representative from each group can then report that group's ideas to the whole class.
3. **Have students discuss the questions in pairs.** This technique encourages the participation of students who are usually too shy to speak in a larger group.
4. **Choose one question and organize a debate on it.** Divide the class into two sections, each of which will prepare arguments for its team.

(*Note:* These suggestions may also be applied to the new What Do You Think? sections.)

Part Two

Some of the exercises in Part Two (such as Glancing at Vocabulary and Discussing the Reading) are similar to those in Part One, and the same teaching suggestions apply. However, the main focus of this part is on finding the main idea of individual paragraphs. Begin by having students skim the paragraphs in the second reading selection and find the main ideas. They should not use the dictionary; rather, they should try to guess the meaning from context. They should not worry about details at this point.

Divide students into small groups to do the new Learning to Summarize section; here, they practice summarizing key information in different paragraphs of the reading. Then each group compares its summaries with those of other groups.

In Chapters Eight to Twelve, students work through the Inferring: Figuring Out the Meaning sections. Completing these exercises requires that students refer back to the reading selection in order to separate ideas *stated* or *implicit* in the reading from those not in it at all.

For the Viewpoint exercises in Chapters Seven, Eight, and Twelve, you can use the techniques suggested for the Discussing the Reading section in Part One. In addition, you might also try a role-play activity where appropriate. Students can play the parts of the different characters from the reading selection.

Part Three

Most the Building Vocabulary and other word study can be assigned as homework. Exceptions are exercises that require students to compete against each other individually or to work together in small groups.

Part Four

As the title Scanning for Information indicates, the ability to find specific information quickly is an important skill for academic students. In chapters with a box containing a short glossary (for example, Chapter Three), go over the key terms with the students. Then have students answer the questions, individually or in groups, from the information found in the realia. Discourage students from reading every word as they hunt for the answers. Instead, they should run a finger over the page (either down or across, depending on the type of realia) until the answer "pops out" at them.

For the Going Beyond the Text section, have students (for homework) find and bring to class maps, brochures, ads, or other related "authentic" materials about a particular chapter theme. As a class or in small groups, share the different materials. The activities in Going Beyond the Text are meant to summarize and extend the ideas and vocabulary from the chapters.

Part Five

The Personal Stories and new What Do You Think? features in this last part provide supplementary reading practice in which students combine and practice the skills learned in other parts of the chapter. Unlike other readings, these may contain a few words and structures not previously introduced. Encourage students to figure out this vocabulary and these forms from context and — if they are not essential to the point — to tolerate ambiguity and to be content to grasp the general

idea. You may want students to tell and/or write their own personal stories — or, in the case of the What Do You Think? boxes, other humorous or interesting jokes, anecdotes proverbs, or stories — relating to the chapter theme and to listen to or to read one another's writing.

New to the Third Edition

1. **Streamlined Design.** The new edition features an attractive two-color design and an extensively revised art program. These changes were initiated to make the books more appealing, up-to-date, and user-friendly. In addition, we made the books easier to use by simplifying complicated direction lines, numbering exercises and activities, and highlighting key information in shaded boxes and charts.

2. **New Chapter Theme on Science and Technology.** The new edition features an entirely new theme for Chapter Eleven: Science and Technology. Some of the latest developments in science and technology and some controversial issues relating to aspects of electronic surveillance and biotechnology are examined. In addition, the themes for several other chapters have been broadened to include new content.

3. **Audio Cassette.** New to this edition is a supplemental audio cassette, containing selected readings from the text. Readings included on the cassette are indicated with a cassette icon in the student text.

4. **What Do You Think?** These new boxed features in each chapter contain interesting short readings such as cartoons, jokes, surveys, and proverbs that present different, often humorous or surprising, points of view on aspects of the chapter themes.

5. **Focus On Testing.** Also appearing in each chapter, these new boxed features focus on specific reading and vocabulary skills designed to help students prepare for standardized tests such as the TOEFL.

Acknowledgments

Our thanks to the following reviewers whose comments, both favorable and critical, were of great value in the development of the third edition of the Interactions/Mosaic series:

Jean Al-Sibai, University of North Carolina; Janet Alexander, Waterbury College; Roberta Alexander, San Diego City College; Julie Alpert, Santa Barbara City College; Anita Cook, Tidewater Community College; Anne Deal Beavers, Heald Business College; Larry Berking, Monroe Community College; Deborah Busch, Delaware County Community College; Patricia A. Card, Chaminade University of Honolulu; José A. Carmona, Hudson County Community College; Kathleen Carroll, Fontbonne College; Consuela Chase, Loyola University; Lee Chen, California State University; Karen Cheng, University of Malaya; Gaye Childress, University of North Texas; Maria Conforti, University of Colorado; Earsie A. de Feliz, Arkansas State University; Elizabeth Devlin-Foltz, Montgomery County Adult Education; Colleen Dick, San Francisco Institute of English; Marta Dmytrenko-Ahrabian, Wayne State University; Margo Duffy, Northeast Wisconsin Technical; Magali Duignan, Augusta College; Janet Dyar, Meridian Community College; Anne Ediger, San Diego City College; D. Frangie, Wayne State University; Robert Geryk, Wayne State University; Jeanne Gibson, American Language Academy; Kathleen Walsh Greene, Rhode Island College; Myra Harada, San Diego Mesa College; Kristin Hathhorn, Eastern Washington University; Mary Herbert, University of California–Davis; Joyce Homick, Houston Community College; Catherine Hutcheson, Texas Christian University; Suzie Johnston, Tyler Junior College; Donna Kauffman, Radford University; Emmie Lim, Cypress College; Patricia Mascarenas, Monte Vista Community School; Mark Mattison, Donnelly College; Diane Peak, Choate Rosemary Hall; James Pedersen, Irvine Valley College; Linda Quillan, Arkansas State University; Marnie Ramker, University of Illinois; Joan Roberts, The Doane Stuart School; Doralee Robertson, Jacksonville University; Ellen Rosen, Fullerton College; Jean Sawyer, American Language Academy; Frances Schulze, College of San Mateo; Sherrie R. Sellers, Brigham Young University; Tess M. Shafer, Edmonds Community College; Heinz F. Tengler, Lado International College; Sara Tipton, Wayne State University; Karen R. Vallejo, Brigham Young University; Susan Williams, University of Central Florida; Mary Shepard Wong, El Camino College; Cindy Yoder, Eastern Mennonite College; Cheryl L. Youtsey, Loyola University; Miriam Zahler, Wayne State University; Maria Zien, English Center, Miami; Yongmin Zhu, Los Medanos College; Norma Zorilla, Fresno Pacific College.

Summary of Reading Skills

Note: All chapters contain practice in the following reading skills/strategies: Preparing to read, getting the main ideas, skimming, recognizing reading structure, guessing meaning from context, understanding details, and learning to summarize.

Chapter	Vocabulary Building	Focus on Testing	Scanning for Information
one	• learning new words by categories • learning new words in phrases	• words in instruction	• a college course catalog
two	• learning new words in categories and phrases • using a dictionary quickly	• synonyms	• a weather report
three	• learning and using words in context	• compound nouns	• food labels
four	• recognizing parts of speech • identifying parts of speech in the dictionary	• identifying parts of speech	• community information (telephone directory, signs)
five	• recognizing parts of speech	• word parts	• housing ads
six	• learning word families	• antonyms	• emergency instructions
seven	• learning and using words with prefixes • reviewing synonyms and antonyms	• recognizing paraphrases	• medicine labels
eight	• learning the meanings of word parts • using a dictionary for definitions and examples	• choosing the correct definition	• TV program guides
nine	• distinguishing between adjectives ending in -*ed* and -*ing*	• easily confused words	• newspaper ads for social activities
ten	• recognizing the appropriate definition	• making analogies	• greeting cards
eleven	• word usage	• homophones	• working with tables
twelve	• compound adjectives	• idiomatic expressions	• magazine ads

CHAPTER one

School Life

in this chapter

You will read about different kinds of international students and look at some aspects of college life in the United States and Canada.

1

International Students in the United States and Canada

Before You Read

Getting Started

Look at the pictures and talk about them.

1. Name the places, things, and people.
2. Describe the pictures. Where is the place? What kind of place is it? Where are the people from? What do they do?
3. How is this place like your school? How is it different?

Interactions I • Reading

Preparing to Read

Think about the answers to these questions. The reading selection will answer them.

1. What are international students? What are resident aliens? What are nonnative speakers of English?
2. Where do most international students go to school?
3. Where do most international students come from?
4. What fields of study are popular with students from other countries?

Glancing at Vocabulary

Here are some vocabulary items from the first reading selection. You can learn them now or come back to them later.

NOUNS	ADJECTIVES	PHRASES
college	popular	nonnative speaker
university	international	field of study
nonresident	practical	
visa	important	
immigrant		
refugee		
citizen		
language		
state		
province		
oil		
country		
fact		

Read the following selection quickly. Then do the exercises after the reading.

International Students in the United States and Canada

A There are many nonnative speakers of English at colleges and universities in the United States and Canada. Nonnatives are usually international students or resident aliens. International students in the United States are nonresidents with F or J visas. Resident aliens are immigrants or refugees. In addition, some U.S. and Canadian citizens are nonnative speakers. They do not speak English as their first language.

B California is the state with the most international students. Texas and New York are next. Other states with large numbers of international students are Massachusetts, Illinois, Michigan, and Pennsylvania. Students from Europe most often attend school in the northeastern or northwestern states, and students from Asia usually go to school in the midwestern and western states. Latin Americans most often study in the South and Southwest, and Africans usually attend school in the Midwest and South. In Canada, many nonnative speakers study in Quebec and speak French. Some go to school in the provinces of Ontario, Nova Scotia, British Columbia, and Alberta.

C Engineering is the most popular field of study for visa students. Many study management and business. Most international students major in practical subjects. These subjects provide useful skills that help students find good jobs.

D Many visa students in the United States come from the Middle East and Asia, and many are from oil countries. Iran, Taiwan, Nigeria, Japan, Hong Kong, Venezuela, Saudi Arabia, China, India, and Thailand send large numbers of students to the United States. International students in Canada often come from Hong Kong, Malaysia, and the United Kingdom.

E Visa students are only a small part of the many nonnative speakers at American colleges and universities. But the facts show that nonnatives are very important in American higher education.

After You Read
Getting the Main Ideas

Write T (true) or F (false) on the lines. The first one is done as an example.

1. __F__ All nonnative speakers of English at American colleges and universities are F or J visa students.

2. _____ All the facts in this reading selection are about international students. They are not about immigrants and refugees.

3. _____ California, Texas, and New York do not have many visa students.

4. _____ Most visa students study practical subjects.

5. _____ Most international students come from Europe.

Guessing Meaning from Context

You do not need to look up the meanings of all new words in a dictionary. You can often guess the meanings of many words from the context.
Sometimes a sentence gives the meaning of a new vocabulary item. The meaning sometimes comes before or after the verb *be*.

example: The context is the words around a new vocabulary item.
(What does <u>context</u> mean? It means <u>the words around a new vocabulary item</u>.)

 **exercise 2** Write the meanings of the underlined words in the following sentences on the lines. The first one is done as an example.

1. <u>International students</u> are nonresidents with F or J visas.

nonresidents with F or J visas

2. <u>Resident aliens</u> are immigrants or refugees.

_____

3. Some <u>Canadian provinces</u> are <u>Ontario</u>, <u>Nova Scotia</u>, <u>British Columbia</u>, and <u>Alberta</u>.

_____

Sometimes the meaning of a new item is in another sentence or another part of a sentence.

example: Most international students major in practical subjects. These subjects provide usefull skills that help students find good jobs.
(What are <u>practical</u> subjects? They are subjects that provide useful skills.)

 **exercise 3**   Find the meanings of the underlined words in the following sentences. Write them on the lines. The first one is done as an example.

1. Students from Europe most often <u>attend</u> school in the northeastern and northwestern states, and students from Asia usually go to school in the Midwest.

   <u>go to</u>

2. Many foreign students study management and business. Most <u>major in</u> practical subjects.

   _____

3. Visa students are only a small part of the many nonnative speakers at colleges and universities. But the facts show that nonnatives are very important in American <u>higher education</u>.

   _____

Recognizing Reading Structure

> Paragraphs divide reading material into topics. One paragraph is usually about one topic. In the reading selection, there is a capital letter next to each of the five paragraphs.

 **exercise 4**   Match each paragraph with its topic. Write the correct letter on the line. The first one is done as an example.

1. __D__ Home countries of international students in the United States and Canada

2. _____ Kinds of nonnative speakers

3. _____ Major subjects of visa students

4. _____ States of the United States and provinces of Canada with many international students

5. _____ Conclusion or summary

Understanding Details

exercise 5

Circle the letters of the *two* correct answers for each blank. The first one is done as an example.

1. Nonnative speakers of English can be _____ .
   a. international students
   b. resident immigrants
   c. U.S. or Canadian citizens with English as a native language

2. Facts on visa students show that many _____ .
   a. attend school in the states of Nevada, Kansas, and Missiouri
   b. from South America study in the southern and southwestern parts of the United States
   c. study practical subjects, like engineering and business

3. Large numbers of visa students come from _____ .
   a. oil countries
   b. Michigan and Pennsylvania
   c. Taiwan, Hong Kong, and Japan

exercise 6

Now turn back to the Preparing to Read section on page 3 and answer the questions.

Discussing the Reading

activity

In small groups, talk about your answers to the following questions.

1. Are you a visa student, immigrant, tourist, or U.S. or Canadian citizen?

2. Which facts in the reading selection are true for you? (For example, are you a European student in a northeastern U.S. state?) How is your situation different from the description in the reading?

3. Which facts in the reading selection are true in your experience? (For example, do most of your nonnative friends study engineering?) Which facts surprise you? Why?

4. In your opinion, why do most foreign students come to the United States or Canada? Why do they prefer certain states or parts of the country? Why do they prefer practical fields of study?

5. Tell the reasons for your choice of state, school, and major subject.

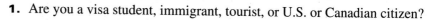

PART two

College Life in the United States and Canada

Before You Read

Glancing at Vocabulary

Here are some vocabulary items from the next reading selection. You can learn them now or come back to them later.

NOUNS		VERBS	ADJECTIVES	PHRASES
campus	homework	lead	undergraduate	take notes
professor	quiz	discuss	graduate	teaching assistants
lecture	test	follow	formal	junior college
discussion	textbook	offer	technical	midterm exam(ination)
seminar	atmosphere	grade	informal	final exam(ination)
instructor	style		available	course outline
classmate	facility		individual	learning center
community	counselor			
certificate	tutor			
degree	recreation			
resident	service			
assignment				

Skimming for Main Ideas

A paragraph usually tells about one topic. Often one sentence is the "topic sentence." It tells the main idea of the paragraph. The topic sentence is often—but not always—the first sentence of the paragraph. The other sentences usually give details or examples to illustrate the main idea.

example: There are several different kinds of classes on university campuses. Professors usually teach large undergraduate classes. They give formal lectures. Students have to listen and take notes. Then teaching assistants (T.A.s) lead discussion groups. In graduate seminars, small groups of students discuss their ideas with their instructor and classmates.

In this example, the first sentence is the topic sentence of the paragraph. It gives the main idea that there are several different kinds of classes on university campuses. The other sentences give examples of these kinds of classes.

Read the following paragraphs quickly. Then underline the topic sentence in each paragraph. The first one is done as an example. Remember that the topic sentence is not always the first sentence.

College Life in the United States and Canada

A   Many native and nonnative students go to community, junior, or technical colleges. All fifty states of the United States and the provinces of Canada have these schools. <u>Community colleges are different from four-year universities in many ways.</u> Some students get a community college certificate or degree after only one or two years of study. Many certificates and degrees are in practical subjects like accounting, business, computer science, engineering, management, and travel. Some students attend a university after one or two years at one of these schools, but many students attend only a community, junior, or technical college. For immigrants, refugees, and citizens, the cost of a community college education is not very high if they are residents of the state. Also, many students at these schools are over twenty-five years old. They work and go to school too. They usually live at home, not on campus. These are only some of the differences between two-year colleges and four-year universities.

B   Instructors at American and Canadian colleges and universities use many different teaching methods. Some instructors give assignments every day. They grade homework. In their classes, students have to take many quizzes, a midterm exam, and a final exam. Other instructors give only writing assignments. Some teachers always follow a course outline and usually use the textbook. Other teachers send students to the library for assignments.

C   The atmosphere in some classrooms is very formal. Students call their instructors "Professor Smith," "Mrs. Jones," and so on. Some teachers wear business clothes and give lectures. Other classrooms have an informal atmosphere. Students and teachers discuss their ideas. Instructors dress informally, and students call them by their first names. American teachers are not alike in their teaching styles.

D   At most American and Canadian colleges and universities, facilities for learning and recreation are available to students. Students can often use typewriters, tape recorders, video machines, and computers at libraries and learning centers. They can buy books, notebooks, and other things at campus stores. They can get advice on their problems from counselors and individual help with their classes from tutors. Students can relax and have fun on campus too. Some schools have swimming pools and tennis courts. Most have snack bars or cafeterias.

After You Read

Learning to Summarize

How can you show your understanding of reading material? You can think about the meaning of the material *in English.* Then you can *summarize* the information in your own words. What is summarizing? It is retelling the main ideas and the important details in short form.

example: Here is a summary of paragraph A of "College Life in the United States and Canada":

Community colleges in the United States and Canada are different from four-year universities. Community college students can get a certificate or degree in a practical subject after one or two years of study. The cost of community college education is not so high for state residents. Many community college students are older. They work, and usually live at home, not on campus.

 **exercise**

Work in groups of three. Choose a different paragraph (B, C, or D) from the reading selection "College Life in the United States and Canada." Summarize the information in your paragraph. Then take turns sharing your summary with your group.

Discussing the Reading

In small groups, talk about your answers to the following questions.

1. Do you attend a community college, a technical school, or a university? What facts in paragraph A are true about your school? What information is not true?

2. Does homework help you learn? Do quizzes help you? Do you want more or less homework in your courses? More or fewer quizzes? Why?

3. Describe the teaching style of your instructors. What style do you prefer? Why?

4. What campus facilities and services does your school have? What facilities and services do you use? Where are they on campus?

PART three

Building Vocabulary

Learning New Words by Categories

> When you read, you can guess the meanings of many words from context. This is one way to learn new vocabulary. Another way to build your vocabulary is to learn new words or phrases by categories or meaning groups. Some examples of categories are "kinds of people," "places," "classroom things," "actions," and so on.
>
> *examples:* <u>People</u>: students, immigrants, refugees, citizens, residents
> <u>Places</u>: community colleges, states, Pennsylvania, campus
> <u>Fields of study</u>: accounting, business, computer science

 **exercise** List the following 15 words by categories: People, Places, Fields of Study. Then add 5 more words of your own to each category.

1. instructor	**6.** counselor	**11.** French
2. Texas	**7.** library	**12.** engineering
3. ESL	**8.** country	**13.** management
4. business	**9.** nonresident	**14.** teaching assistant
5. tutor	**10.** cafeteria	**15.** the Midwest

PEOPLE   **PLACES**   **FIELDS OF STUDY**

_____   _____   _____

_____   _____   _____

_____   _____   _____

_____   _____   _____

_____   _____   _____

_____   _____   _____

_____   _____   _____

_____   _____   _____

_____   _____   _____

_____   _____   _____

Learning New Words in Phrases

> There are many ways to learn new vocabulary words. One way is to learn words by categories of meaning. Another way is to learn words in phrases. A *phrase* is a group of words that belong together, such as an adjective and a noun or a verb and a noun.
>
> *examples:*   Adjective + noun: practical subjects, four-year universities, business clothes
> Verb + noun: attend college, give assignments, take exams

 **exercise 1**   Match the words in column A and column B to make phrases. Write the letters of the words in column B on the lines as in the example.

COLUMN A	COLUMN B
1. _C_ nonnative	**a.** pool
2. _____ a snack	**b.** exam
3. _____ a midterm	**c.** speakers
4. _____ a tape	**d.** of study
5. _____ student	**e.** states
6. _____ a swimming	**f.** counselors
7. _____ a field	**g.** bar
8. _____ northwestern	**h.** recorder
9. _____ higher	**i.** in business
10. _____ a two-year	**j.** a lecture
11. _____ an informal	**k.** education
12. _____ major	**l.** at home
13. _____ give	**m.** college
14. _____ live	**n.** atmosphere

focus on testing

Words in Instructions

Tests often use special words in their instructions. If you want to do well, you have to follow the instructions exactly. Pay special attention to the verbs.

examples: <u>Check</u> the items. = Put a checkmark next to the items.

<u>Discuss</u> the ideas. = Tell your opinions about the ideas.

 **exercise 2**   Match each instruction in column A with the correct example in column B. Write the words from the examples in the blanks. Item 1 is done as an example.

COLUMN A

1. Circle the word. _education_
2. Underline the word. _____
3. Cross out the word. _____
4. Copy the word. _____
5. Count the words and write the number. _____
6. Fill in the blank. _____
7. Complete the word. _____
8. Divide the word with lines.

   _____
9. Write the plural. _____
10. Draw lines and match the words.

    _____
11. Cross out the mistake.

    Correct the word. _____
12. Circle the letter of the correct word.

    _____
13. Number the word. _____
14. Put a check by the word.

    _____

COLUMN B

~~college~~

vocabullalry

<u>resident</u>

academ _ic_

fact, oil, state _3_

your _field_ of study

major _major_

country _countries_

final student
graduate exam

a _____ assignment
    a. grade
    (b.) homework
    c. facility

_4_ visa

_✓_ help

campus

(education)

 **exercise 3**   From column A, Exercise 2, find the verbs that give instructions. Write the verbs on the lines. Two are done as examples.

circle, underline _____

_____

_____

PART **four**

Scanning for Information

A College Course Catalog

Sometimes you need to scan (look for information quickly). Scanning is *not* careful reading.

 **exercise**   Work in small groups. Look at the diagram below and the course descriptions from a college course catalog on page 15. Read the questions on pages 15 to 16. Find the information quickly. Write the answers on the lines. The first group with the correct answers is the winner.

How to Read the Schedule of Classes

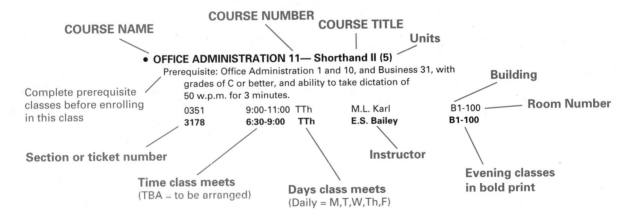

ENGLISH AS A SECOND LANGUAGE

- **ENGLISH AS A SECOND LANGUAGE 3A—GRAMMAR/WRITING**   **6 UNITS**

  Prerequisite: Appropriate score on the assessment test or consent of the instructor.

  Concurrent enrollment in ESL 3B and ESL 3C is strongly recommended.

  | 0227 | 11:00-1:00 | MWF | E.H. Wiskin | A12-103 |
  | **3091** | **7:00-10:00** | **MW** | **A. Tournier** | **CE-221** |

- **ENGLISH AS A SECOND LANGUAGE 3B—READING/VOCABULARY**   **3 UNITS**

  Prerequisite: Appropriate score on the assessment test or consent of the instructor.

  Concurrent enrollment in ESL 3A and ESL 3C is strongly recommended.

  | 0228 | 10:00-11:00 | MWF | E. Hansberry | B1-200 |

- **ENGLISH AS A SECOND LANGUAGE 3C—LISTENING/SPEAKING**   **3 UNITS**

  Prerequisite: Appropriate score on the assessment test or consent of the instructor.

  Concurrent enrollment in ESL 3A and ESL 3B is strongly recommended.

  | 0229 | 9:00-10:00 | MWF | E. Zubrowsky | B1-200 |
  | **5010** | **7:00-10:00** | **TTh** | **C. Schumaker** | **CE-223** |

- **ENGLISH AS A SECOND LANGUAGE 4A—GRAMMAR/WRITING**   **6 UNITS**

  Prerequisite: Completion of ESL 3A with a grade of "C" or better or assessment into ESL level 4. Concurrent enrollment in ESL 4B, and ESL 4C is strongly recommended.

  An intermediate course in oral and written grammar in context, with emphasis on correct sentences and paragraphs.

  | 0230 | 11:00-1:00 | MWF | J.M. Olds | A12-102 |
  | **3094** | **7:00-10:00** | **MW** | **B. Frank** | **CE-224** |

- **ENGLISH AS A SECOND LANGUAGE 4B—READING/VOCABULARY**   **3 UNITS**

  Prerequisite: Completion of ESL 3B with a grade of "C" or better or placement into ESL level 4. Concurrent enrollment in ESL 4A, and ESL 4C is strongly recommended.

  An intermediate course in reading skills and vocabulary, with emphasis on phonics principles.

  | 0232 | 10:00-11:00 | MWF | H. Lannai | A12-102 |
  | **5098** | **7:00-10:00** | **T** | **H.E. Kelly** | **A12-106** |

- **ENGLISH AS A SECOND LANGUAGE 4C—LISTENING/SPEAKING**   **3 UNITS**

  Prerequisite: Completion of ESL 3C with a grade of "C" or better or assessment into ESL level 4. Concurrent enrollment in ESL 4A, and ESL 4B is strongly recommended.

  An intermediate course in principles of good listening, pronunciation, and conversations on everyday topics.

  | 0233 | 9:00-10:00 | MWF | J. Logan | A12-102 |
  | **5011** | **7:00-10:00** | **Th** | **C. Schumaker** | **CE-223** |

---

1. What is the subject for this part of the college course schedule?_____

2. How many English as a Second Language courses are there?_____

    a. How many Grammar/Writing courses are there?_____

    b. How many Listening/Speaking courses are there?_____

3. What language skills do students learn in ESL 3B and 4B?_____

4. What is the name and number of "an intermediate course in reading skills and vocabulary, with emphasis on phonics principles?"_____

5. Which course gives more units of college credit—ESL 3A or ESL 3B?

   _____

6. How many units do students get if they pass ESL 4A and 4C?_____

7. What is a prerequisite?_____

   a. For which course is the prerequisite "Completion of ESL 3A with a grade of 'C' or better or assessment into ESL Level 4?"_____

   b. What is the prerequisite for ESL 3A, 3B, and 3C?_____

   _____

8. What is a section or ticket number?_____

   a. How many sections of ESL 4A are there?_____

   b. What course has the section numbers 0233 and 5011?_____

   c. What are the section numbers of ESL 4B?_____

9. Which two sections meet on Mondays, Wednesdays, and Fridays from 11:00 A.M. to 1:00 P.M.?_____

   a. When do the two sections of ESL 3C meet?_____

   b. How many hours does ESL 4A meet every week?_____

10. How many ESL instructors are there?_____

    a. Which instructor teaches more than one course?_____

    b. Who teaches the morning section of ESL 4A?_____

    c. What does E. Hansberry teach? _____ When?_____

11. How many sections meet in the A12 building? _____

    a. Where does the evening section of ESL 4C meet? _____

    b. Which sections meet in B1-200?_____

12. Which courses do you want to take?_____

    When?_____ Why?_____

    _____

Going Beyond the Text

 **exercise 1**

Here are some kinds of reading material about college life. Check (✓) the kinds available at your school. If possible, bring some examples to class to discuss.

catalog of courses ☐
course schedule ☐
orientation information ☐
campus map ☐
brochures about educational programs ☐
information about facilities and services ☐
school newspaper ☐
other: _____ ☐

 **exercise 2**

Read an article in the school newspaper. Make a list of new vocabulary from the article. Discuss your article with a partner or in small groups.

PART **five**

Personal Stories

Educational Systems

The following three stories give different points of view of college life in the United States.

 **exercise**

Follow these steps for the following stories.

1. Read them quickly and tell the main ideas.
2. Answer your instructor's questions about the stories, or ask and answer questions of your own.
3. Tell your opinions of the ideas in the stories.
4. Tell or write your own story about education or college life.

1   **I**can't stand American college life. I like my teachers and classmates, but I don't like the system of daily classes, assignments, and tests. In my country, students have more freedom and less structure. They don't have to attend lectures or seminars every day. They don't do homework or have quizzes in their courses. They just have to get a certificate of completion for a certain number of courses. The certificate is proof of attendance. After three to five years of attendance, they take final exams. If they pass these important tests, they get a university degree.

2   **I** don't like the teaching style in American college classes. My instructors and classmates are nice, but I can't stand the system of undergraduate education at the university. In my country, students have more structure and less freedom. They have to attend lectures every day and do homework assignments in their textbooks. The professor gives them outlines of the important facts. They have a test and get a grade in every course every week. The questions are multiple choice or fill-in-the-blank, and students just have to choose the correct answer. But in the United States, students take notes, ask questions, and discuss their ideas. I don't like to do those things.

3   **I** think the American system of higher education is too easy. At my community college, many students work, so they don't have much time for homework. They don't know the answers in class, so the instructor teaches the same things again and again. The level of teaching goes down. These students don't study hard for quizzes and exams, so the teacher gives easy tests. We all get good grades, but we don't learn a lot. If students attend class all the time, they usually pass the course and get college credit. After two years, they get a degree. But what does this degree mean?

WHAT DO YOU THINK?

Some kinds of reading have no topic sentence, so you have to figure out the main idea (the point) on your own. For example, a humorous story needs a point to make the story funny. Do you usually understand American humor?

Here and on page 20 are four cartoon stories about the North American educational system. Discuss your answers to these questions:

1. What is the point (the joke) of each cartoon? What idea does the cartoonist want to communicate?
2. Do you think the cartoon is really like school life in the United States or Canada? Is it like school life in your home country? Why or why not?
3. Do you think each cartoon is funny? Why or why not?

DRABBLE By Kevin Fagan

Drabble, reprinted by permission of United Feature Syndicate, Inc.

1.

DRABBLE By Kevin Fagan

Drabble, reprinted by permission of United Feature Syndicate, Inc.

2.

LUANN   **BY GREG EVANS**

Luann, reprinted with special permission of News America Syndicate, Inc.

3.

Drabble, reprinted by permission of United Feature Syndicate, Inc.

4.

CHAPTER **two**

Experiencing Nature

in this chapter

You will read about the effects of weather. You will also learn about camping, a popular leisure-time activity in the United States and Canada. The short stories in the last reading of the chapter give three people's very different opinions about travel and nature.

21

PART ONE

The Powerful Influence of Weather

Before You Read

Getting Started

Look at the pictures and talk about them.

1. Describe the people. What are they wearing? What are they carrying? Why?
2. Describe the kinds of weather. Which kind do you like best? Why?

Preparing to Read

Think about the answers to these questions. The reading selection will answer them.

1. How does the weather affect people's health, intelligence, and feelings?
2. What kinds of weather have an influence on people?
3. What is the "perfect weather"?

Glancing at Vocabulary

Here are some vocabulary items from the first reading selection. You can learn them now or come back to them later.

NOUNS		VERBS	ADJECTIVES	PHRASES
weather	percent (%)	increase	powerful	below average
effect	temperature	relax	strong	on the other hand
health	degree (°)	affect	overweight	air pressure
intelligence	humidity	influence	irritable	
feeling	cause		perfect	
storm	influence			

Read the following selection quickly. Then do the exercises after the reading.

The Powerful Influence of Weather

A **W**eather has a powerful effect on people. It influences health, intelligence, and feelings.

B In August, it is very hot and wet in the southern part of the United States. Southerners have heart attacks and other kinds of health problems during this month. In the Northeast and the Middle West, it is very hot at some times and very cold at other times. People in these states tend to have heart attacks after the weather changes in February or March.

C The weather can also affect intelligence. For example, in a 1938 study by scientists, the IQ [intelligence quotient] scores of a group of undergraduate college students were very high during a hurricane, but after the storm, their scores were 10 percent (%) below average. Hurricanes can increase intelligence. Very hot weather, on the other hand, can lower it. Students in many of the United States often do badly on exams in the hot months of the year (July and August).

D Weather also has a strong influence on people's feelings. Winter may be a bad time for thin people. They usually feel cold during these months. They might feel depressed during cold weather. In hot summer weather, on the other hand, overweight people may feel unhappy. The summer heat may make them tired and irritable.

E Low air pressure relaxes people. It increases sexual feelings. It also increases forgetfulness. People leave more packages and umbrellas on buses and in stores on low-pressure days. There is a "perfect weather" for work and health. People feel best at a temperature of about 64°F with 65 percent humidity (moisture in the air).

F Are you feeling sick, sad, tired, forgetful, or very intelligent today? The weather may be the cause.

After You Read

Getting the Main Ideas

 Write T (true) or F (false) on the lines below and on the next page.

1. _____ The weather influences people's health and feelings.

2. _____ There are the same number of heart attacks in every part of the United States in every month of the year.

3. _____ Intelligence never changes.

4. _____ Hot and cold weather affect all people the same way.

5. _____ Some weather influences are temperature, storms, and air pressure.

6. _____ There is a perfect kind of weather for people's work and health.

Guessing Meaning from Context

> Sometimes a sentence gives the meaning of a new vocabulary item. The meaning or an explanation is sometimes in parentheses ( ), in another sentence, or in another sentence part.
>
> *example:* The IQ scores (measures of intelligence) of a group of under-graduate college students were very high during a hurricane or other kind of storm.
> (What are IQ scores? They are measures of intelligence. What is a hurricane? It is a kind of storm.)

 Write the meanings of the underlined words in the following sentences on the lines. The first one is done as an example.

1. Students often do badly on exams in the hot months of the year (July and August).

   the hot months of the year
   _____

2. People feel best at a temperature of about 64°F (degrees Fahrenheit).

   _____

3. In "perfect weather," the humidity (moisture in the air) is about 65 percent.

   _____

4. Weather has a powerful effect on people. It also has a strong influence on people's feelings.

   _____

5. Thin people might feel depressed during cold weather. Overweight people, on the other hand, may feel unhappy in hot summer months.

   _____

Recognizing Reading Structure

> A reading selection may express one main idea. The main idea includes the topics and ideas of all the paragraphs in the reading. The main idea may be in a topic sentence.

 In the reading selection, there is a letter next to each of the six paragraphs. Match each paragraph with its topic. Write the correct letter on the line.

1. _____ The influence of weather on people's feelings

2. _____ The effect of air pressure on people

3. _____ The effects of heat, cold, and weather changes on people's health

4. _____ Conclusion or summary

5. _____ Introduction

6. _____ The influence of weather on intelligence

 Circle the number of the *one* main idea of the reading.

1. Low air pressure relaxes people.

2. Weather has a strong effect on people.

3. After the storm, people's scores were 10 percent below average.

4. There is a "perfect weather" for work and health.

Understanding Details

 Which *two* answers are correct for each blank, according to the reading selection? Circle the letters.

1. _____ may have a bad effect on health.
  a. Hot, wet weather
  b. Perfect weather
  c. Weather changes
  d. High intelligence

2. Intelligence may increase because of _____ .
  a. storms
  b. very hot weather
  c. a hurricane
  d. low air pressure

3. Low air pressure _____ .
  a. depresses overweight people
  b. relaxes people
  c. increases forgetfulness
  d. causes heart attacks

4. In "perfect" weather of 64°F, _____ .
  a. people are very forgetful
  b. thin people feel cold
  c. people work well
  d. people are in better health

 **exercise 6**   Now turn back to the Preparing to Read section on page 22 and answer the questions.

Discussing the Reading

 **activity**

In small groups, talk about your answers to the following questions.

1. How is the weather in your country? What are the seasons? How and when do they change?

2. Which facts in the reading are true for you? (For example, do you feel more intelligent during storms?)

3. Do you believe that the weather affects health and feelings? Why or why not?

4. What kind of weather is perfect for you? Why?

PART two
Camping

Before You Read
Glancing at Vocabulary

Here are some vocabulary items from the next reading selection. You can learn them now or come back to them later.

NOUNS		VERBS	ADJECTIVES	ADVERBS	PHRASE
equipment	crater	set up	spectacular	especially	in case
insect	ice field	protect	magnificent	fortunately	
hiker	bay	stretch	fascinating		
national park	wilderness	attract	surrounded		
scenery	advantage	spread	breathtaking		
acre	hunting		crowded		
waterfall	solitude		extra		
wildlife	supplies		successful		
volcano	compass				
glacier	facilities				

Skimming for Main Ideas

 **exercise**   In each of the following five paragraphs, there is a topic sentence. It is the most general sentence, and it tells the main idea. Read each paragraph quickly and underline the topic sentence.

Interactions I • Reading

Camping

Camping is a popular form of recreation in the United States and Canada. For most kinds of camping, you need equipment. In this picture, two campers are setting up an umbrella tent. The tent will protect them from the cold, the wind and the rain, and insects. Other people are cooking with a small gas stove. This kind of a camping stove is safe and easy to use. There are two hikers carrying backpacks. Their sleeping bags are light but warm.

The national parks in the United States and Canada offer nature lovers some of the two countries' most spectacular scenery. For example, Yellowstone, the first national park in the world, stretches over 2 million acres from Wyoming into Montana and Utah. It offers magnificent waterfalls, fascinating wildlife, and spectacular geysers. These hot springs throw water out of the ground. In California, Sequoia and Redwood parks attract millions of visitors each year. They go to rest and enjoy themselves among the forests of tall redwood and giant sequoia trees. Another popular national park is Washington state's Mount Rainier. There are glaciers around the crater of this ancient volcano, and fields of beautiful wildflowers surround the crater. The Grand Canyon, in Arizona, is probably the most famous and most popular national park in the world.

Canada's many national parks range from the mountains to the seacoasts. There are snow-covered mountains, ice fields, and blue-green lakes in Banff Park, in the province of Alberta. Not far from Banff is Jasper National Park, almost 3 million acres of breathtaking nature. Newfoundland has Terra Nova, a good fishing area with bays and lakes.

The campgrounds in the popular national parks and forests are often very crowded, especially in spring and summer. Fortunately, wilderness areas offer many advantages to hikers and campers. In these parts of the national park or forest systems, there are no roads, no campgrounds, and no facilities like restrooms or showers, but there *is* great hiking, swimming, fishing, and hunting. And there are not many people enjoying the scenery, the trees and flowers, the wildlife, and the solitude of the wilderness.

E Camping and hiking in wilderness areas can be dangerous, so you must be prepared. You should learn about the area before you go there. You must be in good health, and you must have the right clothing, equipment, and supplies. What if there is a storm? What if you get lost? For possible emergencies of this kind, you should bring extra food and water, a map, and a compass. Careful planning is the key to a safe and successful wilderness trip.

After You Read
Learning to Summarize

How can you summarize the information in a paragraph? First, find the main idea. (The most general sentence, often the topic sentence, may tell the main idea.) Next, find the important details that explain the main idea. (These details may be examples.) Finally, retell the main idea and the important details in your own words. *Remember:* A summary should be *short.*

For example, here is a summary of paragraph A of the reading selection "Camping."

People need equipment for camping. } the main idea

For example, people buy tents, camping stoves, and sleeping bags. } examples

Work in groups of four. Each student chooses a different paragraph (B, C, D, or E) from the reading selection "Camping." Summarize the information in your paragraph. Then take turns sharing your summary with your group.

Interactions I • Reading

Discussing the Reading

In small groups, talk about your answers to the following questions.

1. Do you like camping and hiking? Why or why not?
2. Where do you go camping or hiking? What equipment do you take?
3. What do you do on your camping trips or hikes? What do you see?
4. What do you know about how to plan a safe wilderness trip?

PART three
Building Vocabulary

Learning New Words in Categories and Phrases

> One way to learn new vocabulary is to figure out the meaning from context. You can also build your vocabulary more systematically by learning words in meaning categories and in phrases (groups of words that belong together).

 In each of the following groups, one word does not belong. Cross out the word. To explain your answer, describe the category of the other words. The first one is done as an example.

example: 1. The word *fast* does not belong. The other three words describe kinds of weather.

1. hot	cold	~~fast~~	wet
2. sick	tired	depressed	prepared
3. hurricane	intelligence	humidity	rainstorm
4. crowded	magnificent	beautiful	spectacular
5. lake	river	bay	geyser
6. hot springs	sleeping bag	backpack	tent
7. park	acre	forest	field
8. restroom	solitude	campground	showers
9. rest	enjoy	throw	relax
10. hiking	breathtaking	fishing	hunting

Chapter Two • Experiencing Nature

exercise 2   Follow the instructions for each of the following items.

1. Circle the kinds of weather.

wind   southern   attack   rain   humidity   score   snow   flower   storm

2. Draw a box around the places.

Yellowstone   umbrella   Wyoming   province   hill   Terra Nova

3. Put a check by the living things.

hiking gear   trees   insects   wildlife   plants   temperature

4. Cross out the kinds of scenery.

river   waterfall   field   forest   campfire   solitude   mountains

5. Underline the national parks.

the Grand Canyon   Newfoundland   Sequoia   Mount Rainier   Jasper

exercise 3    Can you make a phrase from the words in each of the following pairs? On each line, write *yes* or *no*. The first two are done as examples.

1. _yes_ cold/weather	**7.** _____ practical/fortunately
2. _no_ native/especially	**8.** _____ set up/forgetful
3. _____ below/average	**9.** _____ magnificent/scenery
4. _____ low/pressure	**10.** _____ recreation/area
5. _____ crowded/campsites	**11.** _____ offer/advantages
6. _____ strong/influence	**12.** _____ restroom/facilities

Using a Dictionary Quickly

When you read, you can often guess the meanings of new words from the context. Sometimes, however, you may need to use a dictionary. With a dictionary, you can find out the pronunciation of words and check the spelling. You can find out parts of speech and check your guesses about meaning. You can find examples of the words in sentences.

In a dictionary, words and phrases (entries) appear in alphabetical order. For example, entries that begin with *a* come before words that begin with all other letters. Entries that begin with *ca* come before words that begin with *ce* or *ci* or *cr*. Entries that begin with *sce* come before words that begin with *sco* or *scr*.

examples:			
1. area	5. fortunately	9. low	13. weather
2. beautiful	6. heart attack	10. lower	14. wet
3. crater	7. ice field	11. measure	15. window
4. degree	8. July	12. moisture	16. windy

Can you find words and phrases in your dictionary quickly? Practice in the use of alphabetical order (forward and backward) will help you. Also, you can use the *guide word* (or *words*) at the top of each dictionary page. The guide word on the left is the same as the first entry on the left-hand page. The guide word on the right is the same as the last entry on the right-hand page.

gear 268		German measles 269

exercise 1 Work quickly. To put the four groups of words below in alphabetical order, number the words in each group from 1 to 8. The first student with the correct answers is the winner.

1.

_____ powerful

_____ influence

_____ camping

_____ affect

_____ health

_____ storm

_____ relax

_____ strong

2.

_____ intelligence

_____ degree

_____ increase

_____ grow

_____ air pressure

_____ attack

_____ feeling

_____ IQ

3.

_____ humidity

_____ hot

_____ hurricane

_____ forgetful

_____ hunting

_____ forest

_____ insect

_____ ice field

4.

_____ magnificent

_____ mountain

_____ monument

_____ wilderness

_____ national

_____ waterfall

_____ weather

_____ modern

 **exercise 2**   Using a dictionary, write the guide words for the page numbers below.

	FIRST WORD	LAST WORD
1. page 215:	_____	_____
2. page 134:	_____	_____
3. page 45:	_____	_____
4. page 178:	_____	_____
5. page 265:	_____	_____

 **exercise 3**   Work quickly. Write the page number and the guide words from your dictionary for each of the following entries. The first student with the correct answers is the winner.

1. tired:	page _____	_____	_____
2. tutor:	page _____	_____	_____
3. scientist:	page _____	_____	_____
4. southern:	page _____	_____	_____
5. pressure:	page _____	_____	_____

 **exercise 4**   Using a dictionary, write 5 pairs of guide words on the lines below. Do not write the page numbers. Then choose a partner and exchange books. Each student writes the page number from his or her dictionary for each pair of words.

1. page _____	_____	_____
2. page _____	_____	_____
3. page _____	_____	_____
4. page _____	_____	_____
5. page _____	_____	_____

exercise 5   For more practice, write your own list of words. For example, list all the new words from Chapters One and Two of this book. Then quickly rewrite the words in alphabetical order. Finally, work fast to find them in a dictionary. For each entry, write the page number and the guide words.

Synonyms

A synonym is a word with the same meaning as another word. For example, *seldom* and *rarely* are synonyms; both words mean "almost never."

Vocabulary tests often include multiple-choice questions about synonyms. One type of multiple-choice question is a sentence with an underlined word or phrase. You read the sentence and then choose which of four words is the closest in meaning to the underlined word or phrase.

example: Hurricanes occur <u>frequently</u> in the Caribbean.

    a. yearly   **c.** quickly

    b. often   **d.** strongly

All four choices make a meaningful sentence, but only one—(b)—often keeps the meaning of the word <u>frequently</u>; only *often* is a synonym of *frequently*.

exercise   Each sentence in 1 to 5 has an underlined word or phrase. Below each sentence are four choices. Choose the one word or phrase closest in meaning to the underlined word or phrase. Circle the letter of the correct answer.

1. I do not have much time for <u>solitude</u> because I am married and have children.
   - **a.** working
   - **b.** seeing friends
   - **c.** being alone
   - **d.** traveling

2. The campers were <u>fortunate</u> because it didn't rain.
   - **a.** safe
   - **b.** happy
   - **c.** dry
   - **d.** lucky

3. Hot weather <u>irritates</u> many people.
   - **a.** burns
   - **b.** kills
   - **c.** relaxes
   - **d.** bothers

4. Weather has a <u>powerful</u> effect on people.
   - **a.** different
   - **b.** dangerous
   - **c.** natural
   - **d.** strong

5. A visit to a national park can be <u>fascinating</u>.
   - **a.** interesting
   - **b.** tiring
   - **c.** irritating
   - **d.** dangerous

PART four

Scanning for Information

A Weather Report

Work in small groups. Look at the weather report from the newspaper. Pretend it is for today's weather. Read the questions on page 35. Find the information quickly. Write the answers on the lines.

City Forecasts

LOS ANGELES: Today—cloudy during morning hours; becoming partly cloudy in afternoon; highs near 80. Tonight—lows 66.

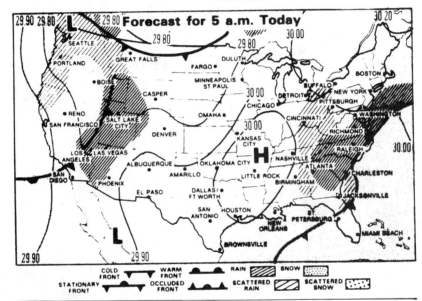

Forecast for 5 a.m. Today

COLD FRONT   WARM FRONT   RAIN   SNOW
STATIONARY FRONT   OCCLUDED FRONT   SCATTERED RAIN   SCATTERED SNOW

Global Report

Gathered by Associated Press for Friday, local time, and by the National Weather Service:

City	Cond.	HI/Lo	City	Cond.	HI/Lo	City	Cond.	HI/Lo
Acapulco	Rain	79/75	Guadalajara	Clear	84/50	Nicosia	Clear	91/63
Amsterdam	Cloudy	63/50	Havana	Cloudy	84/73	Oslo	Cloudy	52/50
Athens	Clear	86/66	Helsinki	Clear	55/36	Paris	Cloudy	70/59
Bangkok	Clear	88/81	Hong Kong	Rain	79/77	Peking	Cloudy	79/55
Barbados	Cloudy	85/75	Jerusalem	Clear	82/61	Rio de Janeiro	Cloudy	82/59
Beirut	Clear	75/64	Johannesburg	Clear	73/52	Rome	Clear	79/64
Belgrade	Clear	81/57	Kiev	Rain	73/54	Sao Paulo	Cloudy	72/57
Berlin	Clear	64/48	Kingston	Fair	91/79	Seoul	Clear	82/55
Bogota	Cloudy	64/45	Lima	Cloudy	70/59	Singapore	Cloudy	90/79
Brussels	Rain	64/50	Lisbon	Cloudy	68/59	Stockholm	Clear	61/32
Buenos Aires	Clear	68/61	London	Cloudy	63/55	Sydney	Clear	75/50
Cairo	Clear	90/64	Madrid	Cloudy	72/50	Taipei	Clear	86/72
Calgary	No report		Manila	Clear	88/73	Tel Aviv	Clear	82/69
Caracas	Cloudy	82/64	Mazatlan	Ptcldy	86/73	Tokyo	Rain	72/64
Copenhagen	Cloudy	63/55	Mexico City	Cloudy	70/53	Toronto	Rain	61/50
Dublin	Rain	57/48	Montreal	Cloudy	68/48	Vancouver	Rain	63/50
Edmonton	No report		Moscow	Clear	68/55	Veracruz	Cloudy	88/72
Frankfurt	Cloudy	70/48	Nassau	Cloudy	90/73	Vienna	Cloudy	63/54
Geneva	Cloudy	55/39	New Delhi	Clear	91/72	Winnipeg	No report	

1. What city of the United States is this newspaper from? How do you know?

   _____

2. Are the temperatures in Fahrenheit or Centigrade (Celsius)? _____

3. Is it cloudy or sunny in Los Angeles today? _____

4. What will the highest temperature in Los Angeles be? _____

5. What do the dark lines on the map of the United States mean? _____

6. Where is it raining in the United States today? _____

7. Where is it snowing? _____

8. What season is it probably? How do you know? _____

9. What is a "global report"? _____

10. Is it raining today in Acapulco, Mexico? _____

11. What is today's high temperature in Berlin, Germany? _____

12. In which Asian cities is it sunny today? _____

    _____

13. Which city has the highest temperature today? _____

14. What kind of weather does your native city probably have today? _____

Going Beyond the Text

 Here are some kinds of reading material about nature. If possible, bring some examples to share with the class (for example, some postcards or information about beautiful places in your home country).

> postcards of scenery ☐
> weather map ☐
> newspaper report ☐
> information about national parks and monuments ☐
> state or province travel brochure ☐
> travel articles in a newspaper ☐
> other: _____ ☐

exercise 2 Read a travel brochure or a travel article in a newspaper. (You can get travel brochures at a travel agency. Many newspapers have special travel sections on Sunday.) Make a list of new vocabulary from the brochure or article. Discuss your brochure or article with a partner.

WHAT DO YOU THINK?

In a humorous story, there is usually a point (a joke). Do you usually understand jokes in English?

Here are two cartoon stories about camping and nature. Discuss your answers to these questions:

1. What is the point of each cartoon story? What idea does the cartoonist want to communicate?
2. Do you think the story could really happen? Why or why not?
3. Do you think each story is funny? Why or why not?

1.

2.

PART five

Personal Stories

Traveling and Nature

The following three stories give different opinions about travel and nature.

exercise

Follow these steps for the stories:

1. Read them quickly and tell the main ideas.
2. Answer your instructor's questions about the stories, or ask and answer questions of your own.
3. Tell your opinions of the ideas in the stories.
4. Tell or write your own story about travel or nature.

1   **I**t's hot and humid in New York City in the summer. The weather has a strong influence on my feelings, and I often feel depressed in July and August. But this summer will be wonderful! My best friend and I are going west. We're going to Wyoming, Utah, Arizona, and New Mexico. We might stay at campgrounds in national parks and forests, but wilderness areas are more fun. We'll ride our dirt bikes in the desert. We can sleep in our sleeping bags and tents and cook on our gas stove. We can take showers in waterfalls and swim in lakes and rivers. We can take beautiful rocks and plants home with us. I believe that natural areas are for recreation. They're there for people to use! So this summer we'll live in nature and enjoy it.

Chapter Two • Experiencing Nature   **37**

2   **M**y friends like to go to the mountains, the desert, and other places with spectacular scenery. They go hiking and camping at campsites. But they also ride dirt bikes, leave their trash in the forest, and take rocks and plants home with them. Then these natural places aren't as beautiful. Don't my friends care about nature? National parks and wilderness areas are places with many kinds of wildlife and plant life. These living things have to survive! Not only people are important to the world—nature is important, too!

3   **W**e all like spectacular scenery, and everyone should see the famous glaciers, volcanoes, giant trees, canyons, waterfalls, and geysers in the national parks of the United States and Canada. But when I travel, I spend most of my time in cities. Why don't I want to live in nature and enjoy it? From my hiking and camping trips, I know that nature doesn't like me! A tent will protect me from the cold, but I have to set it up first, and I can't set up an umbrella tent in a strong wind. A fire will keep me warm, but I can't make a fire in the rain. A backpack with a sleeping bag, a camping stove, and storm gear is heavy! I can't survive in nature. The solitude of the wilderness is for animals and plants, not for me.

CHAPTER three

Living to Eat or Eating to Live?

in this chapter

You will read about the changing eating habits of many North Americans. You will also find out about the relationship between food choices and personality. The last reading selection gives some unusual advice on diet and nutrition.

39

PART ONE

Our Changing Diet

Before You Read

Getting Started

Look at the pictures below and talk about them.

1. Where is the man in each scene and what is he doing?
2. What is the doctor telling the man in the second picture?
3. Do you know anyone like the man? If so, describe the person. Did the person change his or her eating habits? How?

Preparing to Read

Think about the answers to these questions. The reading selection will answer them.

1. Many people in the United States eat a lot of three types of food. What are the types of food, and what are some examples of each type?
2. What is wrong with the typical North American diet?
3. How are some people changing their diet?
4. What types of ethnic restaurants are very popular in the United States and Canada?
5. What kinds of food will we eat in the future?
6. According to the reading selection, what is the key to good nutrition?

Glancing at Vocabulary

Here are some vocabulary items from the first reading selection. You can learn them now or come back to them later.

NOUNS	VERBS	ADJECTIVES	ADVERBS	PHRASE
diet	consist (of)	typical	unfortunately	and so on
fat	reflect	frozen	totally	
cholesterol	include	canned		
substances	prevent	inaccurate		
habit	avoid	growing		
health	achieve	broiled		
vitamin	control	roasted		
protein	limit	high-fiber		
argument				
vegetarian				
alcohol				
relaxation				
caffeine				
garlic				
balance				

Read the following selection quickly. Then do the exercises after the reading.

Our Changing Diet

A **W**hat do most Americans and Canadians usually eat? Many people think that the typical North American diet consists of fast food—hamburgers, hot dogs, french fries, pizza, fried chicken, and so on. They think Americans and Canadians also eat a lot of convenience foods, usually frozen or canned, and junk food—candy, cookies, potato chips, and other things without much nutritional value. Unfortunately, this description is not totally inaccurate. The American diet *is* generally high in sugar, salt, fat, and cholesterol, and these substances can cause health problems.

B However, some people's eating habits are changing. They are becoming more interested in good health, and nutrition is an important part of health. North Americans are eating less red meat and fewer eggs, and they are eating more chicken and fish. Chicken and fish contain less fat than meat and eggs. Many people are also buying more fresh vegetables and eating them raw or cooked quickly in very little water in order to keep the vitamins.

C Restaurant menus are also changing to reflect people's growing concern with good nutrition. The "typical" North American diet now includes food from many different countries. More ethnic restaurants are opening in big cities in the United States and Canada. Foods from China, Japan, Korea, Thailand, India, and the Middle East are very popular. Even fast-food places now offer "lean" (low-fat) hamburgers, broiled or roasted (instead of fried) chicken, and salad bars with a wide variety of fresh fruits and vegetables.

D   How are we going to eat in the future? Because we now know about the importance of nutrition, we will probably continue to eat more fish and vegetables and less meat. We will still buy convenience foods in supermarkets, but frozen foods may be more nutritious and canned foods may have less salt and sugar. Our junk food will not be "junk" at all because instead of candy bars we will eat "nutrition bars" with a lot of vitamins and protein. In the future, our diet will probably be even more interesting and healthful than it is now.

E   In the United States and Canada, food is a very common topic of conversation. People are always discussing new dishes, restaurants, diet plans, and ideas about nutrition. The arguments about the best diets and foods will continue: Are vegetarians really healthy? Is a high-fiber diet with a lot of raw fruits and vegetables better than a diet of cooked foods? Is a little alcohol good for relaxation, or is all alcohol harmful? Is some caffeine good for energy, or is caffeine always bad? Can yellow vegetables really prevent cancer? Will eating garlic help avoid heart attacks? One thing we do know for sure: The key to good nutrition is balance. How do we achieve that balance? We can choose foods from a variety of sources, control the quantities that we eat, limit fats, and exercise.

After You Read

Getting the Main Ideas

exercise **1**   Write T (true) or F (false) on the lines.

1. _____ All North Americans eat only fast food, convenience foods, and "junk food" with a lot of sugar, salt, and fat.

2. _____ People today are becoming more interested in good nutrition and more healthful cooking methods.

3. _____ Foods from other countries are not very popular among North Americans.

4. _____ In the future, people will probably continue to eat more healthful foods.

5. _____ Most people have the same ideas about nutrition.

Guessing Meaning from Context

Sometimes a sentence gives the meaning of a new vocabulary item. Punctuation may give clues to the meaning. A meaning or an explanation is sometimes in parentheses ( ), after a dash (—), or after a comma (,). Sometimes the meaning is in another sentence or sentence part.

examples: Mexican tacos (meat and vegetables in tortillas—a flat kind of Mexican bread) are popular in the southwestern part of the United States. People eat them with salsa, a sauce of tomatoes and spicy chili peppers.

What are tortillas? They are a flat kind of Mexican bread.

What are tacos? They are tortillas with meat and vegetables in them.

What is salsa? It is a sauce of tomatoes and spicy chili peppers.

 *exercise 2* In 1 to 6, write the meanings of the underlined words in the following sentences on the lines. The first one is done as an example.

1. Many people think that the typical North American diet consists of fast food—hamburgers, hot dogs, french fries, pizza, fried chicken, and so on. It also includes convenience foods, usually frozen or canned, and junk food—candy, cookies, potato chips, and other things without much nutritional value.

   fast food: ____ hamburgers, hot dogs, french fries, pizza, fried chicken ____

   convenience foods: _____

   junk food: _____

2. People are eating more chicken and fish—foods without much fat or cholesterol (a kind of fat).

   cholesterol: _____

3. The typical North American diet now includes food from many different countries, ethnic foods.

   ethnic: _____

4. The typical American diet includes convenience foods and junk food without much food value. This choice of food is very high in sugar, salt, and fat, but it does not provide much good nutrition.

   diet: _____

   nutrition: _____

5. Many people are also buying more fresh vegetables and eating them <u>raw</u> or cooked quickly in very little water.

raw: _____

6. Is all alcohol <u>harmful</u>, and is caffeine always bad for the health?

harmful: _____

Recognizing Reading Structure

In the reading selection on pages 41 and 42, there is a capital letter next to each of the five paragraphs. Match each paragraph with its topic. Write the correct letter on the line.

1. _____ Ideas about the typical North American diet

2. _____ Ideas about food and eating habits in the future

3. _____ Discussions about the best diets and foods

4. _____ New types of foods served in restaurants

5. _____ How and why people are changing their eating habits

Circle the number of the *one* main idea of the reading.

1. The typical North American diet now includes food from many different countries.
2. For health reasons, many people are eating more fresh vegetables.
3. Our junk food in the future is not really going to be "junk" at all.
4. North Americans are becoming more interested in good health, and nutrition is an important part of health.

Understanding Details

Connecting words such as *and, but, or,* and *because* often provide clues to the meaning of sentences and paragraphs.

examples: For health reasons, we will continue to eat more fish *and* we may eat less meat. (We will eat more fish for health reasons. We will eat less meat for health reasons. Fish is more healthful than meat.)

We are still going to eat candy bars, *but* they will have a lot of vitamins and protein. (Candy bars do not contain many vitamins or much protein. By contrast, in the future they will contain vitamins and protein.)

At lunchtime, people may eat in a Chinese restaurant *or* they might go to a fast-food place for a Mexican taco. (People might choose between a Chinese restaurant or a Mexican fast-food place.)

People do not want to eat some foods *because* they might cause health problems. (Why don't people want to eat some foods? They might cause health problems.)

 Find the answers to these questions in the reading selection on pages 41 and 42. Write the answers on the lines.

1. What foods are North Americans eating more for better nutrition?

_____

2. What foods are they eating less?

_____

3. Why do people cook vegetables quickly in very little water?

_____

4. What kinds of ethnic foods do North Americans often eat?

_____

5. How will convenience foods change in the future?

_____

6. Why will "junk food" be more healthful?

_____

7. What kinds of questions do people often ask about diets and foods?

_____

 Now turn back to the Preparing to Read section on page 40 and answer the questions.

Discussing the Reading

 In small groups, talk about your answers to the following questions.

1. What was your idea of the typical American diet before your arrival in the United States or Canada? Are your ideas changing?

2. What do you think about fast food, convenience foods, and junk food? Why? Do you have these foods in your country?

3. Can you give some reasons for the changes in the American diet?

4. Do you prefer ethnic restaurants or "typical American" restaurants?

5. What is your idea of good and bad eating habits? Do you have good eating habits? How can you improve them?

PART two
Food Personalities

Before You Read

Glancing at Vocabulary

Here are some vocabulary items from the next reading selection. You can learn them now or come back to them later.

NOUNS	VERBS	ADJECTIVES		PHRASES
personality	express	gourmet	sour	human being
expression	agree	similar	bitter	have in common
café	get along (with)	creative	crunchy	in a hurry
leader		competitive	sweet	astrological sign
		opposed (to)	soft	amusement park
		spicy	bland	cotton candy

Skimming for Main Ideas

 Read the following selection quickly. Underline the topic sentence in paragraphs A to D. Then follow the instructions for section E.

Food Personalities

A   **P**eople express their personalities in their clothes, their cars, and their homes. Because we might choose certain foods to "tell" people something about us, our diets can also be an expression of our personalities. For example, some people eat mainly gourmet foods, such as caviar and lobster, and they eat only in expensive restaurants (never in cafeterias or snack bars). They might want to show the world that they know about the "better things in life."

B   Human beings can eat many different kinds of food, but some people choose not to eat meat. Vegetarians often have more in common than just their diet. Their personalities might be similar too. For example, vegetarians in the United States and Canada may be creative people, and they might not enjoy competitive sports or jobs. They worry about the health of the world, and they are probably strongly opposed to war.

C   Some people eat mostly fast food. One study shows that many fast-food eaters have a lot in common with one another, but they are very different from vegetarians. They are competitive and good at business. They are also usually in a hurry. Many fast-food eaters might not agree with this description of their personalities, but it is a common picture of them.

D   Some people also believe that people of the same astrological sign have similar food personalities. Arians (born under the sign of Aries, between March 21 and April 19) usually like spicy food, with a lot of onions and pepper. People with the sign of Taurus (April 20 to May 20) prefer healthful fruits and vegetables, but they often eat too much. Sagittarians (November 22 to December 21) like ethnic foods from many different countries. Aquarians (January 20 to February 18) can eat as much meat and fish as they want, but sugar and cholesterol are sometimes problems for them.

E   What is your food personality? Take this quiz about North American foods. Circle the letters of the right answers for you.

1. You are at an amusement park, and you want something to eat. Which of these will you buy?
   a. A candy apple
   b. Cotton candy
   c. A vanilla ice cream cone
2. Someone gives you a box of chocolates. Which kind are you going to eat first?
   a. The kind with caramel centers
   b. The kind with fruit centers
   c. The kind with cream centers
3. You are in an Italian café. What do you order?
   a. Espresso
   b. Cappuccino
   c. Milk
4. You are in a movie theater. Which of these will you probably get for a snack?
   a. Nachos
   b. Popcorn
   c. A chocolate bar
5. It's your birthday, and your best friend wants to take you out for dinner at any restaurant you choose. Which of these places are you going to pick?
   a. A Thai or an Indian restaurant
   b. A Mexican or an Italian restaurant
   c. A fast-food place

6. Which do you prefer on most of your sandwiches?
   a. Spicy mustard
   b. Mayonnaise
   c. Butter

7. It's Sunday morning, and you're going to make breakfast. How are you going to cook the eggs?
   a. Eggs rancheros (Mexican style)
   b. Scrambled or fried
   c. Boiled

8. It's early morning. Which of these do you want first?
   a. Black coffee
   b. Orange juice
   c. Hot oatmeal

9. What do you like best on your toast?
   a. Nothing. I like dry toast.
   b. Jelly or marmalade
   c. Butter

10. You're out shopping, and you're hungry. There are only fast-food places in the area. Which will you choose?
    a. A taco place or a Japanese noodle place
    b. A pizza place
    c. A hamburger or a chicken place

Now add up your score:
- For every (a) answer, you get 5 points.
- For every (b) answer, you get 3 points.
- For every (c) answer, you get 1 point.

What is your total score? What does it mean?

If your score is between 40 and 50 points, your food has a strong person-ality—just like you. Your food is sour, spicy, bitter, or crunchy. You are in-telligent and creative.

If your score is between 20 and 40 points, you like many kinds of food. You probably have a strong personality, but you can also get along with many kinds of people.

If your score is under 20, you usually eat sweet, soft, or bland foods, You like to be with people, but you are probably not a leader.

After You Read

Learning to Summarize

How can you summarize a short reading selection? First, tell the main idea (the most general point). Next, tell the main idea of each paragraph. In a very short summary, you can leave out the details that explain the main ideas.

For example, here is the beginning of a summary of the reading selection "Food Personalities."

Our diets can be an expression of our personalities.	The most general idea of the reading selection
For example, some people eat mainly gourmet foods to show they know about the "better things of life."	The main idea of paragraph A
Another example is that vegetarians might have similar personalities.	The main idea of paragraph B

Work in groups of three. Finish the summary of the selection "Food Personalities." One student tells the main idea of paragraph C, another tells the main idea of paragraph D, and the third tells the main idea of paragraph E.

Discussing the Reading

In small groups, talk about your answers to the following questions.

1. What kind of food do you eat most often? Why? Does this kind of food express your personality?

2. Do you know any gourmet eaters? Vegetarians? Fast-food eaters? In your opinion, what kind of people are they?

3. Do you believe the information in this reading and the food quiz? Why or why not?

Compound Nouns

Compound nouns—combinations of two or more words—are very common in English and often appear on vocabulary tests.

examples: grocery store   human being
             bookstore   wildlife

exercise 1   Match the words to form compound nouns, as in the example. (All the words appear in the reading selections in Parts One and Two.) Some words in column B can go with more than one word in column A.

COLUMN A   COLUMN B

1. __j__ amusement   **a.** attack

2. _____ astrological   **b.** bar

3. _____ candy   **c.** candy

4. _____ canned   **d.** chips

5. _____ cotton   **e.** cream

6. _____ diet   **f.** dog

7. _____ fast   **g.** food

8. _____ french   **h.** fries

9. _____ frozen   **i.** market

10. _____ health   **j.** park

11. _____ heart   **k.** plan

12. _____ hot   **l.** problem

13. _____ ice   **m.** sign

14. _____ potato

15. _____ super

16. _____ salad

17. _____ snack

exercise 2   In small groups, write down as many compound nouns as you can think of. The group with the most correct words after ten minutes is the winner.

PART three
Building Vocabulary

Learning and Using Words in Context

If you learn words in meaning categories, you can more easily *use* the words in context in your speaking and writing. You can use many of the words from one category in the same or a similar context.

examples: Category 1 = elements of food (vitamins, minerals, fat, cholesterol, protein, carbohydrates, fiber)

Category 2 = kinds of food (fast food, candy, potato chips, red meat, eggs, tacos, falafel, sushi, and so on)

Context = There is (are) a lot of . . . . . . in . . . . (There

(category 1) (category 2)

are a lot of *vitamins* in vegetables, there's a lot of *fat* in junk food, there's a lot of *cholesterol* in cheese, and so on.)

exercise 1   Work in small groups. From the reading selections in Parts One and Two ("Our Changing Diet" and "Food Personalities"), write as many words and phrases as you can for each of the three categories below. You can also add vocabulary items of your own. The group with the most correct items after fifteen minutes is the winner.

geographical places (countries and states)	places with food	kinds of food
the United States	restaurants	potatoes
Japan	fast-food places	watermelon

 **exercise 2** Finish each sentence below with as many different vocabulary items as you can.

examples:
1. I like to eat <u>potato chips</u>. I don't like to eat <u>broccoli</u>.
2. You can buy food at <u>a snack bar</u>.
3. <u>Wiener schnitzel</u> is a kind of food from <u>Austria</u>.

1. I (don't) like to eat _____ .

2. You can buy food at _____ .

3. _____ is a kind of food from _____ .

PART four
Scanning for Information

Food Labels

 **exercise** Look at the food labels on page 53. Then read the questions on page 54. Find the information as fast as you can. Write the answers on the lines.

Here are some useful words from food labels:

    calories = units of food energy
    serving = average amount of a kind of food for one person for one meal
    gram = a unit of weight
    artificial = not natural
    label = the paper on a food package with nutritional information
    minerals = natural elements in food, such as copper or zinc
    ingredients = things in food
    carbohydrates = elements of food in things like rice, bread, potatoes, and pasta
    additive = an artificial ingredient
    RDA = (recommended daily allowance) the necessary daily amount of a food element one person needs

HOMOGENIZED HALF AND HALF

INGREDIENTS: MILK & CREAM.

NUTRITION INFORMATION PER SERVING

Serving Size ..... ONE HALF CUP (4 fl. oz.).
Servings per Container 4
Calories 160   Carbohydrate .... 5 grams
Protein ... 4 grams   Fat .... 14 grams

PERCENTAGE OF U.S. RECOMMENDED DAILY ALLOWANCES (U.S. RDA)

Protein 10	Vitamin D 4
Vitamin A 8	Vitamin B₆ 2
Vitamin C .... *	Vitamin B₁₂ 6
Thiamine 2	Phosphorus 10
Riboflavin 12	Magnesium 4
Niacin .... *	Zinc 2
Calcium 15	Pantothenic
Iron .... *	Acid 2

*Contains less than 2% of the U.S. RDA of these nutrients.

MJB
ENRICHED LONG GRAIN WHITE
RICE

NUTRITION INFORMATION PER SERVING

SERVING SIZE, RAW	1/6 CUP
SERVING SIZE, COOKED	1/2 CUP
SERVINGS PER PACKAGE	24
CALORIES	100
PROTEIN	2 GRAMS
CARBOHYDRATE	22 GRAMS
FAT	0 GRAMS

PERCENTAGE OF U.S. RECOMMENDED DAILY ALLOWANCES (U.S. RDA)

PROTEIN	4
VITAMIN A	*
VITAMIN C	*
THIAMINE	8
RIBOFLAVIN	*
NIACIN	8
CALCIUM	*
IRON	10

*CONTAINS LESS THAN 2% OF THE U.S. RDA OF THIS NUTRIENT.

MJB LONG GRAIN WHITE RICE IS ENRICHED BY THE ADDITION OF THIAMINE (B₁), NIACIN, AND IRON.

CUT GREEN BEANS
NO SALT ADDED

INGREDIENTS: GREEN BEANS, WATER.
NUTRITION INFORMATION — PER 1/2 CUP SERVING
SERVINGS PER CONTAINER—APPROX. 4

CALORIES	20
PROTEIN	1g
CARBOHYDRATE	4g
FAT	0g
SODIUM	LESS THAN 10mg

PERCENTAGE OF U.S. RECOMMENDED DAILY
ALLOWANCES (U.S. RDA) PER 1/2 CUP SERVING:

VITAMIN A	10
VITAMIN C	6
THIAMINE (VIT. B₁)	2
RIBOFLAVIN (VIT. B₂)	2
CALCIUM	4
IRON	2
PHOSPHORUS	2
MAGNESIUM	2

CONTAINS LESS THAN 2% OF THE U.S. RDA OF
PROTEIN AND NIACIN.
© 1982 DISTRIBUTED BY DEL MONTE CORPORATION
SAN FRANCISCO, CA 94105—PACKED IN U.S.A.
*WT. OF BEANS (8¾ OZ.) BEFORE ADDITION OF
LIQUID NECESSARY FOR PROCESSING

Net Wt ... 16 oz. (1 lb.) 454 g   Cups ... Approx. 2
For good nutrition eat a variety of foods.

MAYONNAISE

NUTRITION INFORMATION PER SERVING

SERVING SIZE	1 TABLESPOON (14 GRAMS)
SERVINGS PER CONTAINER	100
CALORIES	100
PROTEIN	0 GRAMS
CARBOHYDRATE	0 GRAMS
FAT	11 GRAMS
PERCENT OF CALORIES FROM FAT†	99%
POLYUNSATURATED†	5 GRAMS
SATURATED	2 GRAMS
CHOLESTEROL† (50 MG/100 G)	10 MILLIGRAMS
SODIUM (565 MG/100 G)	80 MILLIGRAMS

PERCENTAGE OF U.S. RECOMMENDED DAILY ALLOWANCES (U.S. RDA)

CONTAINS LESS THAN 2 PERCENT OF THE U.S.
RDA OF PROTEIN, VITAMIN A, VITAMIN C, THIA-
MINE, RIBOFLAVIN, NIACIN, CALCIUM, IRON.

†INFORMATION ON FAT AND CHOLESTEROL CON-
TENT IS PROVIDED FOR INDIVIDUALS WHO, ON
THE ADVICE OF A PHYSICIAN, ARE MODIFYING
THEIR TOTAL DIETARY INTAKE OF FAT AND/OR
CHOLESTEROL.

INGREDIENTS: SOYBEAN OIL, PARTIALLY HYDRO-
GENATED SOYBEAN OIL, WHOLE EGGS, VINEGAR,
WATER, EGG YOLKS, SALT, SUGAR, LEMON JUICE,
AND NATURAL FLAVORS. CALCIUM DISODIUM
EDTA ADDED TO PROTECT FLAVOR.

BEST FOODS, CPC INTERNATIONAL INC.
GENERAL OFFICES, ENGLEWOOD CLIFFS, NJ 07632

The Inter-Society Commission for Heart Disease
Resources has recommended that the average
daily intake of cholesterol be reduced to less than
300 mg per day. With only 10 mg per tablespoon,
Best Foods Real Mayonnaise is low in cholesterol.

1. What foods do these labels come from? _____

   _____

2. What things are in a can of green beans? (What are the ingredients?) _____

   _____

3. What are the main ingredients of mayonnaise? _____

   _____

4. What do people probably use half-and-half for? How do you know?

   _____

5. How big is one serving of mayonnaise? _____

6. How many servings are in a can of green beans? _____

7. How much raw rice do you need for one serving of cooked rice? _____

   _____

8. How many calories are in a serving of rice? _____

9. Which of these four foods contains the most calories per serving? _____

   _____

10. What percentage (%) of the RDA of protein is in one-half cup of rice?

   _____

11. How many grams of protein are in one serving of rice? _____

12. How many different vitamins and minerals does the rice contain? _____

13. What chemical additives do you see on these labels? _____

   _____

14. Your doctor says that too much cholesterol is bad for your health. Can you

   eat this mayonnaise? Why or why not? _____

   _____

Going Beyond the Text

 **exercise 1**   Here are some kinds of reading material about food. Can you add some other examples? If possible, bring some examples to share with the class.

labels from food containers (cans, cartons, jars, and so on) ☐

recipes ☐

menus (from restaurants and other eating places) ☐

a diet plan ☐

other: _____ ☐

_____

 **exercise 2**   Read a recipe in a cookbook or magazine. Make a list of new vocabulary from the recipe. Discuss your recipes with a partner or in small groups.

PART **five**
Personal Stories

Food and Dieting

The following three stories give different advice on food and dieting.

 **exercise**   Follow these steps for the stories.

1. Read them quickly and tell the main ideas.
2. Give your opinion of the advice in each story.
3. Give or write your own advice on food or dieting.

1   **M**y doctor has only one diet instruction: If it's white, don't eat it. She says milk from cows is bad for people. (But isn't nonfat milk good? And what about cheese and yogurt?) She says any food with white sugar or white flour is bad for the health. (But we have to eat bread, right?) She says white rice is not as good as brown rice. (How can we eat Chinese food without white rice?) What do you think? I think I need to find a new doctor.

2   *I* love to cook and eat, so I read a lot about food and diet. I like to know the advice and opinion of nutrition experts. For example, one expert says that there is an ideal diet. About fifteen to twenty percent of this perfect eating plan is protein. About fifty to sixty percent is carbohydrates, and about twenty to thirty percent is fat. This nutritionist also says that a high-fiber diet can help prevent cancer. (We can get fiber from foods like bran, nuts, beans, and vegetables.) If we eat a little fish every week, the fish oils may protect us against heart disease. Garlic and onions could reduce the amount of cholesterol in our blood. Do I believe in all this advice? I'm not sure, but I know I love to cook and eat, so. . . .

3   *I* love most kinds of food, but I don't want to gain any weight. Maybe I could even lose a few pounds. Here's some advice from a diet expert:

- Go shopping for food *only* on a full stomach. If you eat before you go to the supermarket, you may not want to buy so much junk food.
- Use a shopping list. Buy *only* the items on that list. Don't take much money when you go food shopping.
- Eat only at a few scheduled times in a few scheduled places, like your kitchen and in restaurants.
- Don't keep candy, cookies, potato chips, soda, or other junk food in the house. And don't eat desserts with a lot of sugar and fat. Eat fruit instead.

I think these are good ideas, but can I do all these things all the time? Could you?

WHAT DO YOU THINK?

Some cartoons have no words. Some have words in speech balloons. Some have captions (the words under the picture). Both the pictures and words express an idea (a joke or a point).
    Pages 57 and 58 have some cartoons about food. Discuss your answers to these questions:

1. What is the point of each cartoon? What idea does the cartoonist want to communicate?
2. Do you think the situation could really happen? Why or why not?
3. Do you think each cartoon is funny? Why or why not?

3.

4.

Getting Around the Community

in this chapter

In what different ways do people in different places give directions? The first reading selection will tell you. Next, you will find out about differences in local laws. Finally, you will read different opinions about Los Angeles, California, the second largest city in the United States.

"How Can I Get to the Post Office?"

Before You Read

Getting Started

Look at the picture and talk about it.

1. Who are the two young travelers? What are they doing? What is their problem?
2. What are the other people in the picture doing?
3. Does this situation ever happen to you? Do you use a map or ask for directions—or both? Do people sometimes ask you for directions? What do you answer?

Preparing to Read

Think about the answers to these questions. The reading selection will answer them.

1. How do people in different places give directions?
2. Sometimes you ask, "How can I get to the post office?" but the person does not know the answer. What might he or she do?
3. How can body language help you?

Glancing at Vocabulary

Here are some vocabulary items from the first reading selection. You can learn them now or come back to them later.

NOUNS	VERBS	ADJECTIVES	PHRASES
rule	carry	confused	ask for directions
travel	find out	flat	get lost
custom	measure	impolite	have a good time
situation	follow		straight down
	lead		have no idea

Read the following selection quickly. Then do the exercises after the reading.

"How Can I Get to the Post Office?"

A   **I** have a special rule for travel: Never carry a map. I prefer to ask for directions. Sometimes I get lost, but I usually have a good time. I can practice a new language, meet new people, and learn new customs. And I find out about different "styles" of directions every time I ask, "How can I get to the post office?"

B   Foreign tourists are often confused in Japan because most streets there don't have names; in Japan, people use landmarks in their directions instead of street names. For example, the Japanese will say to travelers, "Go straight down to the corner. Turn left at the big hotel and go past the fruit market. The post office is across from the bus stop."

C   In the countryside of the American Midwest, there are not usually many landmarks. There are no mountains, so the land is very flat; in many places there are no towns or buildings for miles. Instead of landmarks, people will tell you directions and distances. In Kansas or Iowa, for instance, people will say, "Go north for two miles. Go east, and then go another mile."

D   People in Los Angeles, California, have no idea of distance on the map: They measure distance in Los Angeles in time, not miles. "How far away is the post office?" you ask. "Oh," they answer, "It's about five minutes from here." You say, "Yes, but how many miles away is it?" They don't know.

E   People in Greece sometimes do not even try to give directions because tourists seldom understand the Greek language. Instead, a Greek will often say, "Follow me." Then he'll lead you through the streets of a city to the post office.

F   Sometimes a person doesn't know the answer to your question. What happens in this situation? A New Yorker might say, "Sorry, I have no idea." But in Yucatan, Mexico, not many people answer, "I don't know." People in Yucatan may believe that "I don't know" is impolite. They usually try to give an answer, sometimes a wrong one. A tourist can get very, very lost in Yucatan!

G   One thing will help you everywhere—in Japan, the United States, Greece, Mexico, or any other place. You might not undersand a person's words, but you can probably understand the person's body language: He or she will usually turn and then point. Go in the direction the person points and you may find the post office!

After You Read

Getting the Main Ideas

exercise 1 Write T (true) or F (false) on the lines.

1. _____ Travelers can learn about people's customs by asking for directions.

2. _____ People in different places always give directions in the same way: They use street names.

3. _____ People in some places give directions in miles, but people in other places give directions in time.

4. _____ In some places, people show travelers the way.

5. _____ People never give wrong directions.

6. _____ A person's body language can help you understand directions.

Guessing Meaning from Context

> Sometimes examples of the meaning of a new vocabulary item are in another sentence or in another part of the sentence. The words *for example, for instance,* and *such as* are clues to meaning through examples.
>
> *example:* People in Los Angeles usually talk about <u>distance in time</u>. They'll say things such as, "The post office is about five minutes from here." (An example of <u>distance in time</u> is "five minutes from here.")

exercise 2 Write examples for the underlined words in the following sentences on the lines.

1. In Japan, people use <u>landmarks</u> in their direction. For example, the Japanese will say, "Go straight down to the corner. Turn left at the big hotel and go past the fruit market. The post office is across from the bus stop."

   _____

2. People will tell you <u>directions</u> and <u>distances</u>. In Kansas or Iowa, for instance, they will say, "Go north for two miles. Go east, and then go another mile."

   directions: _____

   distances: _____

Interactions I • Reading

3. You can probably understand a person's <u>body language</u>. She or he will usually turn and then point.

_____

Sometimes details about a vocabulary item give clues to its meaning.

 **exercise 3**   Find the answers to the questions about the underlined word in the following sentences. Write them on the lines.

> In the <u>countryside</u> of the American Midwest, there are not usually many landmarks. The land is very flat, and in many places there are no towns or buildings for miles.

1. What kind of thing is *the countryside*?_____

2. What doesn't it have?_____

3. What does the word *countryside* mean?_____

_____

Recognizing Reading Structure

exercise 4   In the reading selection, there is a capital letter next to each of the seven paragraphs. Write the main topic of each paragraph next to its letter. A and B are done as examples.

A. Introduction _____   **E.** _____

B. Directions in Japan _____   **F.** _____

C. _____   **G.** _____

D. _____

exercise 5   Circle the number of the *one* main idea of the reading.

1. There are not many landmarks in the American Midwest.

2. Never carry a map for travel.

3. There are different ways to give directions in different parts of the world.

4. New Yorkers often say, "I have no idea," but people in Yucatan, Mexico, rarely say this.

Understanding Details

Punctuation often provides clues to the meaning of sentences and paragraphs. A colon (:) or a semicolon (;) can separate two closely related sentences. The second sentence usually explains or adds information to the meaning of the first sentence.

example: In Japan, most streets don't have names; people use landmarks in their directions. (Streets don't have names. For this reason, people use landmarks.)

Commas (,) can separate items in a series.

example: In Japan, people use landmarks in their directions: They talk about hotels, markets, and bus stops. (What are some examples of landmarks? Hotels, markets, and bus stops.)

Quotation marks separate direct quotes (people's exact words) from the rest of the sentence.

example: Instead, a Greek will say, "Follow me." (What does a Greek often say instead of giving directions? "Follow me.")

 *exercise* **6**   Find the answers to these questions in the reading selection on page 61. Write the answers on the lines.

1. The writer of the reading selection has a special rule for travel. What is it?

_____

2. Why are foreign tourists often confused in Japan?

_____

3. What are some examples of Japanese directions?

_____

_____

4. What directions will people give travelers in the American Midwest? (Give examples.)

_____

_____

5. Why don't people in Los Angeles give directions in miles?

_____

6. How do Greeks sometimes give directions? Why?

_____

7. People in Yucatan, Mexico, may give directions differently from people in New York. Explain this statement.

_____

_____

8. How does a person give directions with body language?

_____

_____

 Now turn back to the Preparing to Read section on page 60 and answer the questions.

Discussing the Reading

 In small groups, talk about your answers to the following questions.

1. How do you ask for directions when you're in a new place?

2. How do people give directions in your country?

3. Where do you live now? How do people give directions there?

4. How can you use body language in directions?

5. In your opinion, why do people in different places give directions in different ways?

PART **two**

Different Laws in Different Places

Before You Read

Glancing at Vocabulary

Here are some vocabulary items from the next reading selection. You can learn them now or come back to them later.

NOUNS		VERBS	ADJECTIVES	PHRASES
murder	registration	differ	similar (to)	from one . . . to another
robbery	proof	vary	illegal	vice versa
ticket	insurance	require	legal	against the law
fine	renewal	complain	local	make a turn
crosswalk	liquor	provide	strange	in public
permit			separate	in addition
helmet			smoke-free	

Skimming for Main Ideas

In some reading material, especially the kind in reading-skills textbooks, most paragraphs have a topic sentence. However, in many other kinds of reading, the writer may not use topic sentences. In this case, you have to figure out on your own the main idea, or the point, of each paragraph. One way to do this is to skim the paragraph quickly and decide on the writer's most general point.

 **exercise**

Quickly read each of the following paragraphs and decide on the most general point that the writer wants to make. Then circle the number of the sentence that is the main idea of each paragraph. The first one is done as an example.

Different Laws in Different Places

A

Most major criminal laws in the United States and Canada, such as those against murder and robbery, are similar to those in other countries. Everyone knows these important laws, but immigrants, international students, and travelers may not know about other kinds of laws. Laws may differ from one state or province to another, or even from one city or community to another. Different places may have different laws about driving, drinking alcohol, smoking cigarettes, and so on. An illegal action, for example, in Lima, Peru or Seoul, Korea, may be perfectly legal in Toronto, Canada, or Miami, Florida, and vice versa.

example: Which sentence do you think expresses the main idea?

1. *It is against the law to murder or steal.*
2. *Laws in Korea about smoking and drinking are different from laws in Canada.*
3. *Laws may be different in different places.* ③

B

For instance, in many cities in the United States, it is not legal to jaywalk. This local law may seem strange to visitors. Sometimes they cross a street, and a police officer gives them a ticket. Then they need to pay a fine of $10 to $25 within ten days. They soon learn to cross a street only in a crosswalk or at a corner because it is against the law in that city to cross in the middle of the street.

1. *It is illegal to jaywalk in many American cities.*
2. *Foreign visitors receive a lot of tickets.*
3. *Foreign students think local laws are strange.*

C   At what age can a person drive a car in the United States? The law varies. In some communities, teenagers with driving permits can drive alone after the age of fourteen or fifteen, but only in the daytime; in other places, they can drive only with a licensed driver in the car; in still other places, the legal driving age is sixteen or eighteen. And there are other differences in driving laws. For instance, in some states, drivers can make a right turn after a full stop at a red traffic light, but in other states drivers may turn only at a green light. In many places, but not all places, it is against the law to drive or ride without using a seat belt. Some communities have helmet laws: Motorcycle drivers and bicycle riders have to wear safety helmets. Laws about car registration may vary too: Some communities require proof of car insurance for renewal of car registration, but others don't.

1. *Laws about car registration and driver's licenses are state laws, but laws about seat belts and safety helmets are local laws.*
2. *Driving laws may vary not only from one state to another but from one area to another.*
3. *For safety, it's important to know and follow community driving rules.*

D   Most people know that states in the United States have different laws about the legal drinking age; this age varies, but in most states no one under twenty-one can buy alcohol—even beer or wine. Also, in most U.S. cities, it is illegal to drink alcohol in public. Of course, liquor is legal in restaurants and bars, but it's against the law to drink a can of beer, for instance, on a public street. Some people put the can in a paper bag and drink; nobody can see the beer, but it still isn't legal. In addition, it is illegal to have an open liquor bottle inside a car.

1. *In most American cities, you may drink liquor only in homes, restaurants, and bars.*
2. *It is against the law for people under twenty-one to drink wine.*
3. *States and cities in the United States have different laws about alcohol.*

E   Smoking is no longer legal in many public places, such as airports, eating places, and workplaces. On some international flights, for instance, if one traveler in a row of airplane seats complains about smoking, no person in that row may smoke. On flights within the United States—and on more and more international flights—no one may smoke. Another example is restaurants: Most restaurants in the United States and Canada have separate sections for smokers and nonsmokers, but in some communities, customers may not smoke in *any* restaurants. A third example is offices: In many places, it is against the law not to provide smoke-free office space for workers.

1. *Laws against smoking in public places are becoming more and more common.*
2. *Airplanes and restaurants often have separate sections for smokers and nonsmokers.*
3. *If you don't smoke, you don't have to breathe the smoke from other people's cigarettes.*

After You Read

Learning to Summarize

If there is not much information in a reading selection, the summary may not be much longer than a statement of the main idea. To summarize a short paragraph, add only the main details, such as the important examples.

For example, here is a summary of the first paragraph of the reading selection "Different Laws in Different Places":

Laws may be different in different countries, states or provinces, and cities or communities. Visitors from other places may not know some of the laws about driving, drinking, smoking, and so on.

Work in groups of four. Each student chooses a different paragraph from the reading selection "Different Laws in Different Places." Summarize the information in your paragraph. Then take turns sharing your summary with your group.

Discussing the Reading

In small groups, talk about your answers to the following questions.

1. In your hometown, is it legal to jaywalk? To drive without car insurance? To ride in a car without a seat belt or to ride a motorcycle without a helmet?
2. What is the legal driving age in your city, state, province, or country? The legal drinking age, if any? The legal smoking age, if any?

3. In your community, what actions are against the law in what public places —for example, drinking on a public street, smoking in an eating place?

4. How are some U.S., state, or local laws different from laws in your country? What laws surprise you? Why?

PART three
Building Vocabulary

Recognizing Parts of Speech

When you try to figure out the meaning of a new vocabulary item from the context and to use the item correctly in speaking and writing, it helps to know what part of speech the word is. Sometimes you can tell the part of speech from the *suffix* (the ending) on a word. Here are some common noun and adjective suffixes.

nouns		adjectives	
Suffixes	*Examples*	*Suffixes*	*Examples*
-er, -or, -ist	teach*er*, profess*or*, tour*ist*	-ar	simil*ar*
-sion, -tion	discus*sion*, ac*tion*	-ic, -al, -ical	com*ic*, leg*al*, phys*ical*
-ment, -ness	enroll*ment*, happi*ness*	-ful, -less	health*ful*, hope*less*
-ure, -ture	press*ure*, tempera*ture*	-ive -ical	expens*ive* phys*ical*
-s, -es	state*s*, quizz*es* (plural forms)	-er (than)	high*er* (comparative forms)

exercise 1 Are the following words nouns or adjectives? On each line, write ___n___ (noun) or ___adj___ (adjective). The first three items are done as examples.

1. __n__ speaker
2. __n__ education
3. __adj__ harmful/ harmless
4. _____ management
5. _____ practical
6. _____ popular
7. _____ technical
8. _____ instructors
9. _____ assignments

10. _____ individual
11. _____ competitive
12. _____ nutritionists
13. _____ counselor
14. _____ section
15. _____ creative
16. _____ powerful/ powerless
17. _____ forgetfulness
18. _____ introduction

19. _____ equipment
20. _____ wilderness
21. _____ spectacular
22. _____ expensive
23. _____ temperature
24. _____ travelers
25. _____ beautiful
26. _____ national
27. _____ recreation

exercise 2 Complete the following sentences with the noun or adjective from Exercise 1 that is related to each underlined word. The first one is done as an example.

1. Students study __management__ to become managers.

2. A native _____ of English speaks English as a native language.

3. To become a better reader, you have to practice reading; reading is a _____ skill.

4. Do your instructors assign a lot of homework? Do they give many reading _____ ?

5. Educators try to improve the quality of _____ in schools.

6. Can smoking harm people? Is it a _____ or a _____ habit?

7. Vegetarians are not usually _____ people. They don't like to compete.

8. _____ are experts in nutrition (the study of food and diet).

9. A _____ person likes to create.

10. How can the weather have power over people? Weather can have a _____ effect on people's feelings. People are often _____ against the forces of nature (such as earthquakes, storms, floods.)

11. I often forget things, and I worry about my _____ .

Interactions I • Reading

12. Chapter 3 introduces you to parts of speech. It is a short _____ .

13. _____ are different from tourists; they travel for experience and knowledge more than to see things.

14. My living expenses are high, so I can't buy _____ things.

15. I love _____ scenery; the beauty of nature relaxes me.

exercise **3**

Circle the correct word (noun or adjective) in parentheses. The first one is done as an example.

1. Words appear in a dictionary in (alphabet /(alphabetical)) order.

2. If you study (grammar / grammatical), you learn about parts of speech.

3. Travel is a time for (relaxation / relax) and (recreation / recreate).

4. In Japan, people use landmarks such as buildings in their (directions / directs).

5. The scenery in some areas is (spectacle / spectacular).

6. In Yucatan, Mexico, the (temperature / temperate) is usually high.

7. Do you know the (nation / national) parks of the western United States?

8. In the United States, do you have to fill out a (registration / register) form at the post office if you move to a new community?

9. Is it (legality / legal) in your community to smoke in restaurants?

10. The main idea of a paragraph is more (generality / general) and less (specificity / specific) than the details.

Identifying Parts of Speech in the Dictionary

Each dictionary entry tells you the *part of speech* of the word. Usually, *n* = noun; *v* = verb; *adj* = adjective; *adv* = adverb; *prep* = preposition; and so on. These abbreviations appear *after* the word and the pronunciation and *before* the definitions (the meanings) and the examples.

Some words can be more than one part of speech. In this case, some dictionaries list each as a separate entry. Also, there may be several different definitions for a word within one dictionary entry. Here are examples.

di·rect[1] /dəˈrɛkt, daɪ-/ *v* [T] **1** [*to*] to tell (someone) the way to a place: *I'm lost. Can you direct me to the station?*

direct[2] *adj* **1** straight; going from one point to another without turning aside: *What's the most direct way to get downtown?*

direct[3] *adv* in a straight line; without stopping or turning aside: *The next flight doesn't go direct to Rome. It goes by way of Paris.*

di·rec·tion /dəˈrɛkʃ^un, daɪ-/ *n* **1** [U] the action of DIRECTING[1] (2); control: *The singing group is under the direction of Mr. Blair.*

di·rec·tive /dəˈrɛktɪv, daɪ-/ *n fml* an official order

di·rect·ly /dəˈrɛktliʸ, daɪ-/ *adv* **1** in a direct manner: *He lives directly opposite the church.|She answered me very directly and openly.* —opposite **indirectly 2** at once; very soon: (*infml*) *He should be here directly.*

di·rec·tor /dəˈrɛktər, daɪ-/ *n* **1** a person who directs an organization or company **2** a person who directs a movie or a play, instructing the actors, cameramen, etc.

di·rec·to·ry /dəˈrɛktəriʸ, daɪ-/ *n* **-ries** a book or list of names, facts, etc., usu. arranged in alphabetical order: *The telephone directory*

 **exercise 1**   From the dictionary entries above, copy the parts of speech for these words.

    1. direct _____   **3.** directly_____

    2. direction_____   **4.** director_____

 **exercise 2**   Work in small groups. From your knowledge of grammar and word endings, write the part(s) of speech of each word on the line. Then check your answers in your dictionary.

1. _n_ directions	**6.** _____ straight	**11.** _____ technical
2. _n, v_ answer	**7.** _____ measure	**12.** _____ equipment
3. _____ special	**8.** _____ situation	**13.** _____ permit
4. _____ rule	**9.** _____ tour	**14.** _____ turn
5. _____ travel	**10.** _____ murder	**15.** _____ smoker

exercise 3 From the reading selections in Chapters One to Four of this book, which words are (1) new, (2) difficult, or (3) especially useful for you in your speaking and writing? List the words. After each word, write its part(s) of speech. Then check your answers in a dictionary.

examples: foreign (*adj.*) state (*n, v*) engineer (*n, v*) major (*n, v, adj*)

focus on testing

Identifying Parts of Speech

In Chapter 2, you learned about synonyms. To help you develop your vocabulary and improve your test scores, you should also know about parts of speech.

In addition to multiple-choice questions, you will often find sentence-completion items on tests. With this type of item, you choose words from a list to fill in the blanks in sentences. First, read the sentence carefully and identify the part of speech of the missing word. Then look in the list for a word that correctly completes the sentence.

example: complain follow illegal impolite measure
   require similar strange vary

Laws often _____vary_____ from one state or province to another.

Even if you don't know the meaning of *vary,* you can guess the right answer more easily if you know the part of speech. The blank requires a *verb,* so you have only five words to choose from (*complain, follow, measure, require, vary*).

exercise Complete the following sentences with the displayed words above.

1. An action that is against the law is _____ .

2. Many colleges and universities in the United States and Canada _____ students to study a foreign language.

3. Our neighbors always _____ when we play loud music.

4. We use rulers to _____ short distances.

5. Laws about crime are _____ in most communities, but local laws may differ.

6. Many older people think teenagers are _____ because they don't always say "please" and "thank you."

7. When you go to another country, the customs may seem _____ to you at first.

8. I know a shortcut to the beach, so why don't you _____ me?

PART four

Scanning for Information

Community Information

exercise 1   Look at the pictures. Match the words to the signs. Put the correct numbers on the
signs. The first one is done as an example.

1. Telephone
2. Wet Paint
3. Stop
4. Put Litter Here
5. Ped Xing

6. People Working
7. Keep Off the Grass
8. Beware of Dog
9. Sale! Big Discounts!
10. Restrooms

11. Loading Zone
12. No Fishing
13. Adults Only
14. No Trespassing

Interactions I • Reading

exercise 2

Page 76 has some entries from the Community Services section of a local telephone directory. (The names of the services and the telephone numbers for your community are probably different.) When might someone need to call one of these numbers? Work in small groups. Read the situations below. Imagine you are in each situation and decide which service you should call. Look at the entries on page 76 and then write the letter of the entry on the line.

1. _____ Someone in your family has an alcohol problem. He drinks too much and causes trouble.

2. _____ You need to renew your driver's license and your car registration.

3. _____ Your friend wants to take college courses, but she can't enroll in a four-year university.

4. _____ You want brochures about tourist places in your community for visitors from your home country.

5. _____ Your friend is HIV positive. You want information about AIDS prevention.

6. _____ You are a visa student, but you want information about immigration to the United States.

7. _____ Because of drinking in a public place and drunk driving, someone in your family has a legal problem. She needs low-cost advice.

8. _____ You can't find a place to live. You think it's because apartment owners don't like your family.

9. _____ You are having family problems, but you want your family to stay together. You'd like low-cost help.

10. _____ You want more information about your community and about travel in the area, but you don't want to buy expensive books.

A | AIDS/HIV

Aid for AIDS.............................213-656-1107
AIDS Education & Prevention Center..213-636-6296
AIDS Epidemiology Program..............213-351-8196
AIDS Project Los Angeles (APLA)........800-922-2437
Or..213-876-2437
Multilingual.................................800-922-2438
Spanish....................................800-400-7432

B | ALCOHOL & DRUG ABUSE

Adult Children of Alcoholics (ACA)......818-342-9885
Al–Anon..................................213-387-3158
Spanish...................................310-948-2190

C | CHAMBERS OF COMMERCE

Beverly Hills............................310-271-8126
Brentwood...............................310-476-4573
Century City.............................310-553-2222
Culver City...............................310-287-3850

D | COUNSELING

California Self-Help Center
Statewide referrals to support groups.........800-222-5465
Family Service
Los Angeles..............................213-381-3626
Los Angeles Free Clinic..................213-653-1990

E | DEPARTMENT OF MOTOR VEHICLES

Culver City 11400 W Washington Blvd.....310-271-4585
Hollywood 803 N Cole Ave.....................213-744-2000
1600 Vine St................................213-461-6257
Santa Monica 2235 Colorado Ave...........310-271-4585

F | COMMUNITY COLLEGES

Los Angeles City College
855 N Vermont Ave, Los Angeles.............. 213-953-4000
TDD...213-351-8196
Santa Monica College
1900 Pico Blvd, Santa Monica...................310-450-5150
TDD...310-452-9273
West Los Angeles College
4800 Freshman Dr, Culver City..................800-400-7432

G | HOUSING

California State Dept. of Fair
Employment & Housing 213-897-1997
TDD...213-897-2840
InfoLine-Information & Referrals For Emergency
Assistance...........................213-686-0950

H | IMMIGRANT & REFUGEE SERVICES

Immigration Legal Assistance Project..213-485-1872
U.S. Immigration & Naturalization Service
Information & Forms..................213-894-2119
  Or...800-755-0777

I | LEGAL SERVICES

American Civil Liberties Union-ACLU..231-977-9500
Bet Tzedek Legal Services...................213-939-0506
Los Angeles County Public Defender...310-491-6361
Malibu..................................... 310-317-1348
Santa Monica...........................213-653-1990

J | LIBRARIES

Brentwood - Bookmobile.......................310-575-8016
Culver City - 4975 Overland Ave.............310-559-1676
Malibu
Main 23519 W Civic Center Way...............310-456-6438

TDD stands for Telecommunications Devices for the Deaf.

Going Beyond the Text

exercise 1

Work in small groups with a local telephone directory. For the ten situations in Exercise 2 on page 75, write the name and telephone number of a community service place (or the names of several places) in your community.

COMMUNITY SERVICE PLACE (AGENCY, ORGANIZATION, ETC.)	TELEPHONE NUMBER
1. _____	_____
2. _____	_____
3. _____	_____
4. _____	_____
5. _____	_____
6. _____	_____
7. _____	_____
8. _____	_____
9. _____	_____
10. _____	_____

exercise 2

For several days, read all the signs on your way to and from school or work. Write down the words from some of the signs that are new or unfamiliar. Bring your list of words to class. Discuss their meaning with a partner or in small groups.

PART five

Personal Stories

Los Angeles, California

The following story tells about different opinions of one of the largest and most famous cities in the world.

 *exercise*

Follow these steps for the story:

1. Read it quickly and tell the main ideas.
2. Make two lists of the important details: (a) bad things about Los Angeles and (b) good things about Los Angeles.
3. What good and bad things do people sometimes say about your community or city? Make two lists.
4. Tell or write about your own community or city.

I live in the second-largest city in the United States—Los Angeles, California—but nobody seems to like my city! Here are some of the terrible things that people say about L.A.

- A British visitor: "Los Angeles is just a collection of ugly villages."
- A German tourist: "San Francisco is like a European city, but L.A. is just Disneyland."
- Visitors from Denver, Colorado: "The sky is blue and the air is clear in our mountain city—not like in smoggy L.A."
- Visitors to national parks in the area, even the Grand Canyon: "The smog in these spectacular places comes from L.A."
- A famous actor from New York: "There is only one good thing about L.A.—drivers can make a right turn at a red traffic light."
- A sign in San Luis Obispo, a town on the California coast: "Smile! You are 192 miles from L.A."
- Residents of San Diego, California (about 100 miles south of L.A.), don't want the Los Angeles area to get bigger. They are afraid their city will become "Los Diego."

- Phoenix is a fast-growing city in Arizona, a state next to California. Now they are having more and more crime problems, like shootings on the freeway. They call these crimes "L.A.-style shootings."
- The four seasons in most places in the United States and Canada are summer, fall, winter, and spring. In Los Angeles, people say the four seasons are drought, fire, flood, and earthquake.

Some people won't come to Los Angeles for a visit. Other people come, but they complain all the time! But I love L.A., so I have some questions for the complainers:

- If Los Angeles is so ugly, why do people make so many movies here?
- If visitors want to see pretty villages and European-like cities, why do they come to the United States?
- Who doesn't like Disneyland?

There are many good things about L.A. Here are some of them:

- Beautiful weather
- Beaches and the ocean
- Ethnic communities
- Many kinds of restaurants
- Scenery and recreation areas
- Entertainment
- Movie stars

WHAT DO YOU THINK?

Here are some very old laws from communities in the United States. Most people have never heard of these laws, so nobody tries to change them. Discuss your answers to these questions:

1. Why do you think the state or city has each of these laws?
2. Why does each law seem funny today?

- A resident of Walden, New York, can't give a traveler a glass of water without a permit.
- In Carrizozo, New Mexico, it's illegal to not shave. (This law is for men *and* women.)
- A police officer in Omaha, Nebraska, is breaking the law if he puts his hands in the pockets of his uniform.
- In Kentucky, it is against the law to carry an ice cream cone in your pocket.
- In Dyersburg, Tennessee, no woman may ask a man for a date on the telephone.
- In Ohio, don't put your feet out the car window. It's against the law!

Interactions I • Reading

Home

in this chapter

What comes to mind when you think of a family? If your idea of a family is a mother, a father, and a few children, the information in the first reading selection may surprise you. In the second selection, you will read about how many families in the United States spend—and used to spend—their evenings at home. Finally, you will read stories about two very different housing situations.

PART **one**

The Changing Family

Before You Read

Getting Started

Look at the pictures and talk about them.

1. Where and when does (did) each scene take place? What are the people doing?
2. How are these scenes similar to ones in your native country? How are they different?
3. Is your family similar to any family in the pictures?
4. How do you think family life is changing these days?

Preparing to Read

Think about the answers to these questions. The reading selection will answer them.

1. What is the difference between an extended family and a nuclear family?
2. What are some kinds of families in the United States today?
3. Why did the structure of the family start to change in the early 1900s?
4. Why were the 1930s and 1940s difficult years for most American families?
5. How did people's ideas about marriage and family change after World War II?
6. What is the most common family structure in the United States today?

Glancing at Vocabulary

Here are some vocabulary items from the first reading selection. You can learn them now or come back to them later.

NOUNS	VERBS	ADJECTIVES	PHRASES
decade	decline	alive	live under the same roof
widow	rise	biological	grow up
rate	face	previous	fall into
divorce	double	childless	
generation	triple	typical	
suburbs	quadruple		

82   Interactions I • Reading

Read the following selection quickly. Then do the exercises after the reading.

The Changing Family

A At the beginning of the twentieth century, many people thought that the American family was falling apart—in other words, they thought it was dying. A century later, we know that this was not the case. However, although the family is still alive in the United States, its size and shape are very different from 100 years ago.

B In the late 1800s and early 1900s, there were mainly two types of families in the United States: the extended and the nuclear. The extended family usually includes grandparents, parents, and children living under the same roof. The nuclear family consists of only parents and children. As people began to move to other parts of the country to find better jobs, the nuclear family became the most common family structure, or unit.

C Today there are many different kinds of families. Some people live in "traditional" families, that is, a stay-home mother, a working father, and their own biological children. Others live in two-paycheck families (where both parents work outside the home), single-parent families (a mother or father living with the children), adoptive or foster families (where adults take care of children that are not biologically theirs), blended families (where men and women who were married before marry again and combine the children from previous marriages into new families), childless families, and so on.

D What caused the structure of the family to change? In the early 1900s the birthrate began to decline and the divorce rate began to rise. Women were suddenly choosing to go to college and take jobs outside the home.

The 1930s and 1940s were difficult years for most families in the United States. Many families faced serious financial, or money, problems during the Great Depression, when many people lost their jobs. During World War II (1939–1945), 5 million women were left alone to take care of their homes and their children. Because many men were at war, thousands of these "war widows" had to go to work outside the home. Most women worked long hours at hard jobs, especially in factories.

E   During the next decade, the situation changed. There were fewer divorces, and people married at a younger age and had more children than the previous generation. It was unusual for a mother to work outside the home during the years when her children were growing up. Families began leaving cities and moving into single-family homes in the suburbs. The traditional family seemed to be returning.

F   In the years between 1960 and the 1990s, there were many important changes in the structure of the family. From the 1960s to the early 1970s, the divorce rate doubled and the birthrate fell by half. The number of single-parent families tripled, and the number of couples living together without being married quadrupled.

G   There are many people today who would like the "traditional" family to return. However, less than 10 percent of families in the 1990s fall into this category. In fact, the single-parent household—once unusual—has replaced the "traditional" family as the typical family in the United States. If we can judge from history, however, this will probably change again in the twenty-first century.

After You Read

Getting the Main Ideas

exercise 1

Write T (true) or F (false) on the lines.

1. _____ Families in the United States today are generally smaller than they used to be.

2. _____ The 1930s and 1940s were good years for most Americans.

3. _____ The typical family of the 1970s was very similar to the typical family of the 1950s.

4. _____ There are more two-paycheck families in the United States today than any other kind of family.

Guessing Meaning from Context

As you learned in Chapter Three, sometimes an explanation or a synonym of a new vocabulary item is in another part of the sentence and is set apart by punctuation. Besides punctuation, the phrases *in other words* and *that is* (abbreviated *i.e.*) are clues to the meanings of words and expressions. The word *or* is another clue that an explanation or meaning will follow.

example: Many people live in two-paycheck families; that is, both parents work outside the home. (What is a <u>two-paycheck</u> family? It's a family where both parents work outside the home.)

 On the lines, complete the explanations or definitions of the underlined words in the following sentences.

1. Many people thought that the American family was <u>falling apart</u>; in other words, they thought it was dying.

   Falling apart in this sentence means _____

2. Some people live in <u>traditional families</u>, that is, a stay-home mother, a working father, and their own biological children.

   A *traditional family* consists of _____

3. The nuclear family became the most common family <u>structure</u>, or unit.

   Structure in this reading is a synonym of_____

4. Many families faced <u>financial</u>, or money, problems during the Depression.

   If you have *financial* problems, you probably don't have much _____

Recognizing Reading Structure

 In the reading selection, there is a capital letter next to each of the seven paragraphs. Match each paragraph with its topic. Write the correct letter on the line.

1. _____ Why the nuclear family became common in the United States

2. _____ Changes in the family structure after World War II

3. _____ The family in the twenty-first century

4. _____ Introduction to the topic

5. _____ Changes in the family since 1960

6. _____ Why the structure of the family changed in the United States during the first half of the twentieth century

7. _____ Types of families that exist today

 Circle the number of the *one* main idea of the reading.

1. The structure of the family changes when women work outside the home.

2. Because of economic changes, the nuclear family became the main family structure in the United States.

3. Family structure in the United States changed several times in the past century and will probably continue to change in the next century.

4. There are more single-parent families than any other kind of family in the United States today.

Understanding Details

> When you read about history, it is important to understand when things happened. In other words, you need to be able to recognize the *chronological order* of events (the time that things happened). One way to do this is to look for key words and phrases.
>
> *examples:* General time clues (words like *first, second, then,* and *finally*)
>
> Specific time clues (words that name dates—*September 8;* years—*1960s/1995*; days—*Thursday*; and times—*6:45 A.M.*)

 Match the events in column A with the years in column B. (You will use some years more than once.) Find the answers in the reading selection on pages 83 and 84. Write the correct letters on the lines.

COLUMN A

1. _____ Many families had money problems.

2. _____ The single-parent home became the most common family structure.

3. _____ Families started moving to the suburbs.

4. _____ The Great Depression and World War II.

5. _____ The divorce rate fell.

6. _____ The birthrate began to fall.

7. _____ The nuclear family replaced the extended family as the most common family structure.

8. _____ Many women went to work in factories.

COLUMN B

a. early 1900s
b. 1930s–1940s
c. 1950s
d. 1990s

 **exercise 6** Turn back to the Preparing to Read section on page 82 and answer the questions.

Discussing the Reading

activity In small groups, talk about your answers to the following questions.

1. Do you live alone, in a small family group, or in an extended family? What is the main family structure in your home country?

2. In your opinion, what is the main reason the family changed after the 1950s? Explain your answer.

3. What do you know about the Great Depression? Do you know anyone who lived in the United States during the 1930s and 1940s? What was life like?

4. Has you native country ever been involved in a war? Describe how people's lives change during a war.

5. In your opinion, how and why might the structure of the family change in the twenty-first century?

PART two

Evenings with the Family—Present and Past

Before You Read

Glancing at Vocabulary

Here are some vocabulary items from the next reading selection. As you read the selection, try to guess the meanings of the new words from the context. Use your dictionary only when absolutely necessary.

NOUNS	VERBS	ADJECTIVES	ADVERB	PHRASES
loser	argue	quiet	hardly	"boob tube"
argument	disappear	pleasant		center of attention
snack	rock			back and forth
porch	reappear			social center
breeze				for a moment
pipe				small talk
fan				
pause				

Skimming for Main Ideas

Read the following selection quickly. Then circle the number of the main idea of each paragraph.

Evenings with the Family—Present and Past

A **W**hat happens in the typical American home every evening after dinner? First, everyone argues about who is going to do the dishes. Then the loser of the argument goes into the kitchen while the rest of the family disappears into the living room, the family room, or even their own rooms. They will spend the next several hours sitting there. They may make a quick trip to the kitchen for a snack sometime during the evening, but other than that they hardly move. Even if two or more family members are in the same room, they are quiet; nobody says much to anyone. What are they doing? They're watching TV. All evening long, the "boob tube" is the center of everyone's attention.

1. *Americans argue about the dishes because nobody likes to do them.*
2. *In many families, there is a TV set in more than one room.*
3. *Because of television, family members don't share activities or talk.*

B When I was a child, we used to spend hot summer evenings on the front porch of our house. We didn't have air-conditioning, so the house was always too warm after dinner; but there was usually a cool, pleasant breeze out on the porch. We children used to play games or read comic books there while my father sat in his rocking chair and rocked back and forth for hours. Sometimes he smoked his pipe or did the crossword puzzle from the newspaper. Mother used to use a paper fan when there was no breeze. Sometimes she cleaned strawberries. Then, later in the evening, she took them into the kitchen and reappeared in a few minutes with big dishes of strawberries and cream.

1. *The front porch used to be a nice place for the family in the summer.*
2. *The front porch was always cool in the summer.*
3. *My parents liked to relax on the porch after dinner.*

c   The front porch was also a kind of social center. There were special "rules" for evenings on the porch. Everyone knew the rules, but nobody said anything about them. For example, when people in our town took walks on summer evenings, they often stopped for a moment at the bottom step of our porch. This pause was almost a social rule; it was like a knock on the front door. Then my father always said, "Come on up and sit down!" This was another "rule": He always used those exact words. Then Mother brought out lemonade or iced tea—never coffee or juice or alcohol. Everyone talked about the local baseball team, gardening, and the hot weather; we children learned our first lessons in small talk on the porch.

1. *People talked only about important things on our porch.*
2. *There were certain social "rules" on the front porch.*
3. *We never used to drink coffee or alcohol.*

After You Read

Viewpoint

> In many reading selections, authors give their point of view (or opinion) about the topic. Sometimes an author's viewpoint is stated directly, but more often it is only implied (suggested).

exercise 1 What is the author's viewpoint in the reading selection on pages 88 and 89? Does she tell you directly what her opinions are, or does she only suggest them? Below, circle one of the words in parentheses.

 1. I believe that the author (likes / dislikes) evenings at home in front of the TV set.

 2. She (liked / disliked) summer evenings on the front porch when she was a child.

exercise 2 Work in small groups. Explain your answers in Exercise 1. Give reasons from the reading.

Learning to Summarize

> A good summary of a paragraph consists of the main idea with the important "specific details," such as *examples* of the main idea.

exercise 3 Work in groups of three. Each student chooses a different paragraph from the reading selection on pages 88 and 89. Summarize the information in your paragraph. Then take turns sharing your summary with your group.

Discussing the Reading

activity In small groups, talk about your answers to the following questions.

 1. What does your family usually do in the evenings after dinner? Is this typical in your home country? Was it typical twenty years ago?
 2. Do you watch much TV? What do you think about television?
 3. Is there a special "social center" in your home? Where is it? What do you do there?
 4. How old do you think the author was when she wrote the reading selection? Why do you think that?

PART three
Building Vocabulary

Recognizing Parts of Speech

As you know, to figure out the meaning of a new word, it is useful to know what part of speech the word is. Page 91 has more common suffixes that will help you recognize words by their parts of speech.

Interactions I • Reading

nouns		adjectives		adverbs	
Suffixes	Examples	Suffixes	Examples	Suffixes	Examples
-ance -ence	dist*ance* differ*ence*	-ant -ent	dist*ant* differ*ent*	-ly	clear*ly* simp*ly*
-ty -ity	abili*ty* availabil*ity*	-able -ible	avail*able* respons*ible*	-ally	scientific*ally*

exercise 1   Are the following words nouns, adjectives, or adverbs? On each line, write __n__ (noun), __adj__ (adjective), or __adv__ (adverb). The first one is done as an example.

1. __n__ intelligence   7. _____ available   13. _____ community
2. _____ importance   8. _____ politely   14. _____ responsible
3. _____ creativity   9. _____ personality   15. _____ responsibility
4. _____ pleasant   10. _____ directly   16. _____ identity
5. _____ magnificent   11. _____ quickly   17. _____ equivalent
6. _____ magnificence   12. _____ convenience   18. _____ truly

exercise 2   Fill in the chart with the missing parts of speech. Use a dictionary if you need help. (Some of the suffixes you will use are from Chapter Four.) The first one is done for you.

nouns	adjectives	adverbs
1. _intelligence_	intelligent	_____
2. responsibility	_____	_____
3. _____	active	_____
4. _____	traditional	_____
5. _____	_____	importantly
6. happiness	_____	_____
7. _____	pleasant	_____
8. perfection	_____	_____
9. typicalness	_____	_____
10. _____	_____	recreationally

Word Parts

Some vocabulary tests ask you to fill in missing parts of words. Some-times these missing parts are suffixes.

example: Our instruct_or_ this year is very interesting. She comes from Australia.

You probably know from your study of vocabulary that the suffixes *-er, -or,* and *-ist,* when added to verbs, form a noun that means "a person who. . . ." To get the example correct, you had to remember the noun *instructor.*

exercise   Read the following sentences. Most of the sentences have at least one incorrect word. Write the part that is missing. If you think a word is complete and doesn't need any-thing, put an X in the blank.

1. People from differ_____ cultural backgrounds may think different_____ about family life. For instance, there may be a big differ_____ in their ideas about the import_____ of marriage and children_____ .

2. Family members today may not share many family activit_____ because they probably lead very act_____ lives outside the home. For example, a woman may active_____ run her own business. In this case, she probably expects her family to take more responsibil_____ for housework and shopping .

3. Nobody in our family likes to clean up the kitchen after dinner. I guess we're a typical_____ American family. My brother and I had a terrible argu_____ last night about the dish_____ . Final_____ , after about ten minutes of screaming, we decided to do them together. Unfortunate_____ , my brother and I are both care_____ people. We broke three glass_____ and a very expens_____ plate.

PART four

Scanning for Information

Housing Ads

 Look at the following classified ads (advertisements) for different kinds of hous-
ing. Then read the statements about the ads on pages 94 and 95. Check (✓) all the
true statements. Use the list of abbreviations to help you. Find the information as
fast as you can. The first ad is done as an example.

Common abbreviations in rental ads:

+ = and
air = air conditioning
ba = bathroom
bch = beach
bd (or bedr) = bedroom
blk = block
bltins = built-ins (the
    refrigerator and
    stove are already
    there)
frplc = fireplace
furn = furnished (the apart-
    ment has furniture)
gt = great
htd = heated
ins = insurance
lg = large
loc = location
m/f = male or female
nu cpts/drps = new carpets and
    drapes
priv = private
rec = recreation

sec bldg = secured building
    (has locks or a
    guard at the main
    entrance)
sgl (or bach) = single (or bachelor)
    apartment; there
    is no bedroom;
    instead the sofa
    in the living
    room becomes
    a bed
stv/ref
(or stv/frig) = stove/refrigerator
unf = unfurnished (the
    apartment does
    not have furniture)
util = utilities (gas, elec-
    tricity, water)
w/ = with
wk = week
yd = yard

1. This ad is for an apartment with

    a. _____ furniture.

    b. _✓_ carpets and drapes.

    c. _✓_ a stove and refrigerator.

    d. _____ one bedroom.

    e. _✓_ rent of $290 per month.

2. This building

    a. _____ has some single apartments.

    b. _____ has some one- or two-bedroom apartments.

    c. _____ has furnished apartments.

    d. _____ has new carpets and drapes.

    e. _____ has a stove and refrigerator.

    f. _____ is a good place for a child.

3. This building

    a. _____ has one-bedroom apartments for $355 per month.

    b. _____ is near shopping areas.

    c. _____ is a safe (security) building.

    d. _____ is good for a person without a car.

4. This building

    a. _____ has two-bedroom apartments for $590 per month.

    b. _____ seems to have many apartments.

    c. _____ has apartments with fireplaces.

    d. _____ allows dogs and cats.

    e. _____ has a heated pool.

    f. _____ has a gymnasium.

5. This motel offers

    a. _____ free rent.

    b. _____ cable television.

    c. _____ no bathroom and no telephone.

    d. _____ room cleaning.

6. These rooms

    a. _____ are in small apartments.

    b. _____ don't have bathrooms.

    c. _____ don't allow pets.

    d. _____ are probably for one person.

7. A person in this living situation

    a. _____ gets living space and food.

    b. _____ has to work.

    c. _____ needs an insured car.

    d. _____ can smoke in the home.

8. These places may be expensive because they

    a. _____ are in security buildings.

    b. _____ are very big.

    c. _____ include luxuries.

    d. _____ are near the beach.

    e. _____ are beautifully furnished.

Hotels & Motels

● CULVER CITY ●
• FREE MOVIE CHANNEL •
$15 OFF FIRST WEEK
$130/WK & UP, PHONE, PRIV BATHS, QUIET, REFRIG, LAUNDRY, MAID SERVICE, SECURITY BLDG.
3927 VAN BUREN, 555-1058

Rooms

CHEVIOT Hills, fab lg house, big bdrm, huge ba, clean, bright, cheery, cat ok $575 555-1307

PRIV entry w/patio, rm/ba in Cent C home. Student employed female $398 555-9854

Room & Board

WESTWD Exchange for Driving kids, etc. 3-7pm Mon-Fri. Must provide car/ins. N/S. 555-9973

Unfurnished Houses

MALIBU $3100mo Incl util, 3000' Pt Dume home, priv bch access, 818/555-0071

MANHATTAN Bch $3200 Ocean View, 4 bdrm, 3 ba, family rm + wet bar, office, 2 firepls, Pool & spa. No pets. 555-9365

Going Beyond the Text

exercise **1**

Work in small groups with the housing section of your local newspaper. Work as quickly as possible to find the best ad for each of the following five situations. Circle and number each ad (1, 2, 3, etc.) or cut it out. Talk about your reasons for each choice.

    1. You are single, and you need the least-expensive place available. Size doesn't matter, but it has to be within walking distance of your school.

    2. You are a single parent with a six-year-old child. Your son stays with you during the week but goes to his other parent on weekends and during the summer. He has a dog. You want a nice place for him and you, but it can't be expensive.

3. You are an unmarried couple, and you want to live together. When you were children, you both lived in friendly neighborhoods. Your houses had front porches and gardens. You remember those times, and you want to live that way again.

4. You and your husband have four children of different ages. They all like television, but they also have their own lives and need their own space. The family has enough money for a house with a yard.

5. You just got divorced. You want to meet many single people and invite new friends to your beautiful home. You don't care about the price.

 Write a classified ad for the place where you live (or for a place where you'd like to live). Discuss your ad with a partner or in small groups.

PART five
Personal Stories

Housing

The following stories tell about two very different housing situations.

 Follow these steps for the stories.

1. Read each story quickly and tell the main idea.
2. Answer your instructor's questions about the stories, or ask and answer questions of your own.
3. Tell your opinions of the ideas in the stories.
4. Tell or write aboutyour own housing situation.

1

Our New Home

My family and I lived in an apartment until last spring. We weren't happy there. The building was crowded and noisy, and the manager didn't use to fix things. We decided to move. But most available apartments in this city were even worse, and the rent was higher. So we started to look for a house to buy.

It was very difficult to find a house! Homes in quiet, pleasant neighborhoods were too expensive. We found a few inexpensive houses, but the areas were dangerous. Prices in all areas seemed to go up every day, and we needed to find a place fast. We began to get nervous.

Finally, my husband and I found a small house in a neighborhood that wasn't bad. The problem was the house itself. It was ugly. It needed paint.

Interactions I • Reading

The wallpaper was horrible; there were scenes of hunting and fishing all over the bedroom walls! The carpet was in terrible condition, and it was *orange*. The porch and roof needed repairs. The "garden" consisted of dirt, weeds, and a few half-dead plants with insects all over them. When our kids first saw their new home, they burst into tears. I understood that. I wanted to cry too.

Well, the four of us made a decision to share the work and spend our summer vacation on the house. We cleaned up the yard and painted the house. We fixed the porch and roof. We removed the ugly wallpaper and carpet. We planted trees and grass. Day by day, this horrible little house became our *home*. We're happy here. The kids are content—except for one thing. Now it's their job to cut the grass every weekend.

2

No Home At All

My father died when I was three years old, and I didn't have a happy childhood. I left home when I was sixteen. My sister and mother moved to another state, so I never talk to them anymore. I'm forty years old now, and I live on the streets.

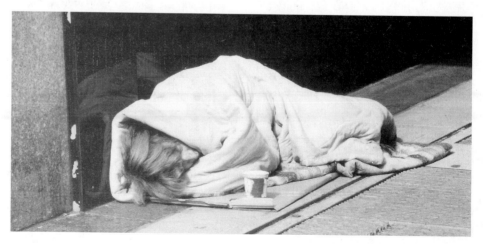

I used to be married, but my wife divorced me because of my alcohol problem. I lost my job and never found another one. After a while, I didn't have any money for rent, so I lost my apartment too. Now I sleep outside in quiet areas of the city. People call me "the Can Man" because I collect empty cans and bottles early in the morning. I sell the cans and bottles and buy food and other things with the money.

About a year ago, I decided to write a book about the experiences of a homeless man. My English isn't very good, so I needed to take some English courses. After I saved enough money, I registered for a course at the local community college. Now I write during the day and study English at night. If my book is good, I may not be homeless for much longer. I don't need a fancy home, but I miss sleeping in a bed with a roof over my head.

WHAT DO YOU THINK?

People often think and talk about "the old days" with their families—when they were children, when they lived on a farm or in a small town, and so on. Here are some memories of people of different ages. Read them, then discuss your answers to these questions:

1. What time (the 1940s, the 1950s, the 1960s, etc.) do you think each memory is from? What place is the memory from? Why do you think so?
2. From the story, do you think family life at that time was better or worse than family life today? Why?
3. Do you have any memories like these? Do these stories bring back other memories? Explain.

1 When I was a child, prices were very, very low. Meat and cheese cost about 25¢ a pound, and a pound of potatoes was only 2¢. My mother could buy a dress for $1.95 and a pair of shoes for $1.79. Furniture and toys were cheap too. But most families didn't buy many new things because only the men worked outside the home, and they didn't make much money. A shopping trip took a long time—we had to look for bargains!

2 There was television, but my family didn't have a set. My parents used to turn on the radio every evening after dinner because their favorite shows were on. They used to laugh at the "Eddie Cantor Show," the "Amos 'n Andy Show," and other radio personalities. We children never understood the jokes. But we liked the afternoon radio shows for boys. While we listened, my brother and I used to draw pictures. My sister used to play with paper dolls.

Chapter Five • Home

3   **M**y father was a busy farmer, but he had time for fishing too —especially when it was windy or cloudy. He thought the fishing was better then. He taught my brothers and me all about fishing. It was simple—a long pole, string, a hook, and fresh worms from our backyard!

4   **I** remember the cold winters—especially the snow. In our small town, there was no school when there was a snowstorm. We stayed home and played. My mother used to cook wonderful hot soup and bake cookies on those days. When we got in her way, she used to dress us in heavy, warm snowsuits and send us outside. We had snowball fights and made a snowman.

CHAPTER six

Emergencies and Strange Experiences

in this chapter

Do you like to read murder mysteries? Some people can solve the mystery long before the story ends. There is a mystery story in two parts in this chapter. Read it and find out if you are a good detective. The final reading sections contain stories about emergencies and strange events that really happened— believe it or not!

PART one

A Murder Mystery: The Critic in the Storm

Before You Read

Getting Started

Look at the picture and talk about it.

1. What kind of story is this scene from?
2. What happened to the man on the floor? How does he look?
3. Who is the man by the door? How does he feel?
4. Who is the other man? What is he doing? How does he feel?

Preparing to Read

Think about the answers to these questions. The reading selection will answer them.

1. Who was Edward Grimsley? What was he doing at the beginning of the story?
2. Who came to see him late one night? Why? What was the problem?
3. Who was Ambrose Pennwright? How did he die?
4. What did Grimsley see in Pennwright's room?

Glancing at Vocabulary

Here are some vocabulary items from the first reading selection. You can learn them now or come back to them later.

NOUNS	ADJECTIVES	VERBS	ADVERB	PHRASES
detective	well-known	hit	nervously	at the height of
guest	heavy	chase		face down
article	loud	shake		butter knife
evidence		bite		out of place
		lie		

Read the following selection quickly. Then do the exercises after the reading.

A Murder Mystery: The Critic in the Storm

A **E**dward Grimsley, the world-famous detective, was spending his vacation on a small Caribbean island. There were beautiful beaches and facilities for water sports and other recreation near his hotel. In addition, at Grimsley's hotel there was a meeting of people in the restaurant business. Thus, because Grimsley enjoyed good food almost as much as he enjoyed a good mystery, the island was the perfect place for Grimsley's vacation. The only disadvantage was the time of year: the hurricane season.

B On Grimsley's second night at the hotel, a powerful storm hit the sleepy little island. Strong winds and heavy rains chased the tourists inside, and as a result most people were sitting nervously in their rooms. Therefore, Grimsley was surprised by the knock on his door at 11:00 P.M., at the height of the hurricane.

C The hotel manager was standing there. He looked worried. His hands were shaking, and he was biting his lip. The wind outside was very loud; thus, when he spoke, he had to shout.

D "Mr. Grimsley," he said, "we have a problem here at the hotel. I know this is your vacation, but you are a detective, and I hope you can help us. A hotel guest died this evening: Mr. Ambrose Pennwright."

E "The famous food critic?" asked Grimsley. "Well, well. Mr. Pennwright is—er, *was*—quite well-known for his newspaper articles about restaurants. This is very interesting. How did he die?"

F The manager shrugged his shoulders and looked a little lost. "Of course," he said, "it's possible that he had a heart attack. But I'm afraid that possibly someone murdered him. The telephone lines are down from the storm, so we can't call the police yet. Can you help us?"

G Grimsley followed the manager to the room of the unfortunate restaurant critic to examine the evidence. Ambrose Pennwright's very large body was lying face down on the floor next to a small table. A bottle of wine, a glass, a plate with cheese, some caviar, and a butter knife were on the table, but there did not seem to be a gun, a sharp knife, or any other weapon anywhere. Nothing in the room seemed out of place, but Grimsley felt there was something strange about the atmosphere. He examined the body for a minute, and he saw that Pennwright was not bleeding. There was a very small piece of caviar on the critic's lower lip.

H   "Who found the body?" Grimsley asked the manager. "And who last saw him alive?"

I   "Please come with me," the manager said. "There are several people in my office. You ought to discuss the situation with them."

to be continued . . .

After You Read

Getting the Main Ideas

Write T (true) or F (false) on the lines.

1. _____ The main character, Edward Grimsley, works at a famous hotel.

2. _____ The story starts during a terrible snowstorm.

3. _____ During the storm, one of the hotel managers died.

4. _____ The police came a few minutes after someone from the hotel called them.

Guessing Meaning from Context

Sometimes words in other sentences or in another part of the sentence are clues to the meaning of a new vocabulary item.

example: Edward Grimsley was spending his vacation on a small Caribbean <u>island</u>. (Here are the clues to the meaning of the word *island*: It is small, it is in the Caribbean Sea, and people can spend their vacations on it. Therefore, an island is a place—a small piece of land in the middle of water.)

The questions after each of the following sentences will lead you to clues to the meaning of the underlined words. Find the answers in the reading selection and write them on the lines. Then circle the letter of the words that give the correct meaning of the underlined vocabulary items.

1. Edward Grimsley was spending his vacation on a small Caribbean island. There were beautiful <u>beaches</u> with facilities for water sports near his hotel.

Where was Grimsley spending his vacation? _____

What is an island?_____

What activities are common near *beaches*?_____

What are *beaches*?
a. mountains for vacations
b. places near the sea
c. hotels for detectives

2. There was a small piece of <u>caviar</u> on the critic's lower <u>lip</u>. The nervous hotel manager was biting his lip.

What part of your body has an upper and a lower section? _____

What does a person bite when he or she is nervous?_____

What is a *lip*?
a. part of the mouth
b. part of the leg
c. a kind of food

Where was the piece of *caviar*? _____
What is *caviar*?
a. a kind of clothing
b. blood
c. a kind of food

3. "How did he die?" asked Grimsley. The manager <u>shrugged his shoulders</u> and looked a little lost.

What are *shoulders*?_____

When did the manager *shrug his shoulders*?_____

_____

Did he know the answer to Grimsley's question? How do you know?_____

_____

What does *shrug one's shoulders* mean?
a. It is a movement of the body. It means "I don't know."
b. It is an answer to a question. It means "I'll tell you later."
c. It is an action. It answers a question about directions.

exercise 3   Which words in each of the following sentences give clues to the meanings of the underlined words? Circle the words. Then circle the letter of the word or words that give the correct meaning of the underlined vocabulary item. The first one is done as an example.

1. The wind outside was very (loud;) thus when he (spoke,) he had to shout.
    a. speak loudly
    b. sing
    c. explain the situation

2. He looked worried. His hands were shaking, and he was biting his lip.
    a. relaxed
    b. nervous
    c. hungry

3. "The world-famous food critic?" asked Grimsley. "He was quite well-known for his newspaper articles about restaurants."

    world-famous:
    a. traveling around the world
    b. known everywhere
    c. knowing everything about restaurants

    food critic:
    a. a person who does not like food
    b. a person who reads the newspaper
    c. a person who writes about restaurants

4. There did not seem to be a gun, a sharp knife, or any other weapon anywhere.
    a. a kind of knife or gun
    b. a mystery
    c. something used to hurt or kill

5. He examined the body for a minute, and he saw that Pennwright was not bleeding.
    a. looked at
    b. listened to
    c. talked to

6. "Who found the body, and who last saw him alive?"
    a. a weapon
    b. a dead person
    c. a living person

Recognizing Reading Structure

> In a fictional story (a story that didn't really happen), the events may not appear in exact chronological order (*first, second, third, fourth, next, then,* and so on). For instance, the main event of a mystery story, such as a murder, may happen outside the story. Also, the people in the story may tell about events that happened earlier.
>
> *example:* At the height of the hurricane, the hotel manager knocked at Edward Grimsley's door. He said, "A hotel guest died this morning." (Which came first? The beginning of the hurricane or the guest's death? The writer didn't say. But the hotel manager went to Grimsley's room after those two events.)

 **exercise 4**
Here are all the important events from the mystery story so far. What happened first? Second? Third? Fourth? Next? After that? To show the chronological order of the events, write the numbers 1 to 8 on the lines, as in the example below.

_____ A hurricane hit the island.

_____ The manager told Grimsley about the death of Ambrose Pennwright.

_____ The manager wanted Grimsley to talk with some other people in his office.

_____ Grimsley, a famous detective, went to a Caribbean island for a vacation.

_____ The hotel manager came to see Grimsley during the storm.

_____ Grimsley examined the evidence—the room and the dead body.

__1__ Mr. Ambrose Pennwright used to write newspaper articles about restaurants.

_____ Someone brought wine, cheese, and caviar to Mr. Pennwright's room.

Understanding Details

> Transitional words often provide clues to the meaning of sentences and paragraphs. The following words and expressions have similar meanings: Like the connection word *so,* they all show an effect.
>
> | | | |
> |---|---|---|
> | therefore | consequently | because of this |
> | thus | as a result | for this reason |
>
> *example:* There were beautiful beaches and facilities for water sports; <u>thus</u>, it was a perfect place for a vacation. (Because there were beautiful beaches and facilities for water sports, it was a perfect place for a vacation.)

 Find the answer to each of the following questions in the reading selection. Write the answers on the lines.

1. Why were the tourists sitting nervously in their rooms?

   _____

2. Why was Grimsley surprised by the knock at the door of his hotel room?

   _____

3. Why was the hotel manager shouting at Grimsley?

   _____

4. Why didn't the hotel manager call the police?

   _____

exercise 6 Complete the following sentences. Circle the letters of *all* the correct answers for each blank.

1. Edward Grimsley _____ .
   a. was a detective
   b. enjoyed good food
   c. enjoyed mysteries
   d. was in the restaurant business
   e. was on vacation

2. The advantages of the Caribbean island were _____ .
   a. the beaches
   b. the time of year
   c. the receational facilities
   d. a hurricane
   e. the meeting of people in the restaurant business

3. Perhaps Ambrose Pennwright _____ .
   a. was still alive
   b. killed someone
   c. had a heart attack
   d. died because someone killed him
   e. died of a gunshot from the gun on the table in his room

4. Ambrose Pennwright was _____ .
   a. a detective
   b. dead
   c. famous as a food critic
   d. a small man
   e. bleeding

5. In Pennwright's room, Grimsley _____
   a. saw things out of place
   b. found the murder weapon
   c. felt something strange about the atmosphere
   d. called the police
   e. saw a piece of caviar on Pennwright's lip

 Turn back to the Preparing to Read section on page 102 and answer the questions.

Discussing the Reading

 In small groups, talk about your answers to the following questions.

   1. In your opinion, why was the hotel manager worried?
   2. How many clues to Pennwright's death can you find? What are they?

PART two

A Murder Mystery (continued)

Before You Read

Glancing at Vocabulary

Here are some vocabulary items from the next reading selection. You can learn them now or come back to them later.

NOUNS	VERBS	ADJECTIVES		ADVERBS	PHRASES
owner	cry	silent	probable	terribly	gourmet restaurant
chef	notice	calm	honest	silently	TV program (show)
	introduce	poor	afraid		drinking problem
	hate	natural	angry		
	taste				

Skimming for Main Ideas

Read the following selection quickly. Then circle the number of the one main idea of each section.

A Murder Mystery (continued)

The manager led the detective to his office. Inside, there were two men and a woman. They were silent.

Althea Pennwright, Ambrose's widow, was not crying. In fact, she seemed quite calm and relaxed. She offered Edward Grimsley her hand.

"You're going to find my husband's murderer," she said. "How nice."

Next, Grimsley met Gregory Welles. Welles was the owner of a famous gourmet restaurant in New York.

"Ambrose Pennwright was my best friend," Welles said, "and his murder is terribly unfortunate." Grimsley noticed a pleasant expression on Welles' face. There was no sign of sadness.

Then the manager introduced Grimsley to Horace Goodbody, a vegetarian chef with his own television program called "How to Cook for Health."

"Ambrose was like a brother to me," Horace Goodbody said. "He got me the job on my TV show. I hope you find the killer soon." Goodbody's expression was similar to the widow's and the restaurant owner's; he didn't appear to be upset.

1. *Althea Pennwright was Ambrose's widow.*
2. *Gregory Welles owned a gourmet restaurant in New York.*
3. *Horace Goodbody had a TV show about vegetarian cooking.*
4. *The three people in the hotel office did not seem upset about Ambrose's murder.*

Grimsley shook his head. "I'm confused," he said. "You're all talking about the *murder* of poor Mr. Pennwright, but nobody is sure it was murder. Possibly he died of natural causes."

Althea Pennwright stood up. Her face became hard and unpleasant. "A natural cause is possible, but I think murder is more probable. Do you want the truth? Everyone hated my husband. He was rich, intelligent, and powerful, but he was a terrible person. None of us is upset about his death. Unfortunately, we all have our reasons . . ."

Grimsley waited silently for a moment.

"Gregory Welles, for example, was afraid of my husband," Mrs. Pennwright continued. "The food in Mr. Welles' restaurant looks and tastes wonderful, but the quality is very poor. It contains chemicals and is worse than junk food. My husband found out and was writing an article about it when he came here."

Welles stared at her unhappily.

"Horace Goodbody," she continued, "is not an honest person. He has a very popular TV program. Every vegetarian in America watches it. However, in real life, Horace's diet consists mainly of fast food. His diet is not healthful. In fact, he isn't even a vegetarian. My husband was planning to tell the world about Mr. Goodbody in his next article. Horace knew this; thus, he was afraid of losing his TV show."

W

Goodbody had an unhappy expression on his face.

X

"And you, Mrs. Pennwright?" Mr. Grimsley asked. "Why did you hate your husband?"

Y

"Why did I hate my husband?" Mrs. Pennwright repeated. "He had a terrible personality. We were always arguing because we had nothing in common. I wanted to see a marriage counselor, but he wouldn't even talk about it."

Z

"He had a drinking problem. Because of his job, he was always eating. He became terribly overweight. Yes, I hated him."

1. *The detective was confused about the three people in the office.*
2. *The three people all hated Ambrose Pennwright for different reasons.*
3. *Gregory Welles was afraid of Ambrose Pennwright because the food in Gregory's restaurant was not very good.*
4. *Horace Goodbody ate unhealthy fast food; he was rich and powerful.*

AA

She stared straight into Grimsley's eyes. "However," she said, "I did not kill him. When I last saw him, he was eating some cheese, drinking some wine, and reading a magazine. I left the hotel room and was watching TV and talking with Mr. Goodbody in the bar all evening. Then Mr. Welles ran in and told us about Ambrose."

BB

"Aha!" said Grimsley. "You found the body, Mr. Welles?"

CC

"Yes," Welles said. "I was walking past the Pennwrights' room when I heard a low voice inside: Someone needed help! The door was locked. After I tried for about five minutes to open it, I finally broke down the door. Unfortunately, I was too late. There was Ambrose on the floor—dead. He way lying on top of his magazine. I ran to the hotel manager, and he went to you. Then I went into the bar, told Mrs. Pennwright and Mr. Goodbody about the murder, and we came to this office."

DD

"Hmmmm. . . ." Grimsley walked slowly back and forth for several minutes. Then he stopped.

EE

"Aha!" he finally shouted. "I know the answer to this mystery—the murderer and the murder weapon! I am quite sure that . . ."

1. *From the evidence and the suspects' (possible murderers') stories, the detective figured out the answer to the mystery.*
2. *Mrs. Pennwright and Mr. Goodbody spent the whole evening together.*
3. *Gregory Welles found Ambrose Pennwright's body and told everyone about the murder.*
4. *Ambrose Pennwright called for help before he died.*

After You Read

Solving the Mystery

exercise 1 A good reader is like a good detective. Read the story again and look for clues (pieces of information that lead to the solution to a mystery). Then answer the following questions.

1. Paragraph G on pages 103 and 104 contains the physical evidence of the mystery. What are all the possible clues? _____

   _____

   _____

2. In paragraphs AA and CC on page 111, Mrs. Pennwright and Mr. Welles tell their stories. What was in their stories but not in the picture on page 102?

   _____

   What was in the picture but not in their stories? _____

3. When two ideas are *contradictory,* one idea has to be false if the other idea is true. Often in a mystery story, one or more suspects is lying (not telling the truth). There is contradictory information in paragraph C on page 103 and in paragraph CC on page 111. What is the contradiction? _____

   _____

   Who is probably lying?_____
   Why? _____

4. What two facts from paragraph G on pages 103 and 104 and paragraph M on page 110 might go together? _____

Learning to Summarize

A summary of a story (true or fictional) is different from a summary of a paragraph. When you summarize a story, tell only the important events in chronological order. If there are important details, include them in your sentences about the events. For example, here is a summary of the beginning of the story "The Critic in the Storm."

> Edward Grimsley, a famous detective, was vacationing on a Caribbean island. During a hurricane, a restaurant critic—Ambrose Pennwright—died. When the hotel manager asked for Grimsley's help, the detective examined the room and the dead body.

The summary of a mystery story also includes information about the suspects and their motives (possible reasons) and the important clues that lead to the solution.

exercise 2

Work in groups of four. In paragraph form, each student answers one of the following questions. Your answers, in order, will be a summary of the story "The Critic in the Storm."

1. What important events happened in the story?

2. Who were the suspects and what were their possible motives for the murder?

3. What were the important clues to the mystery?

4. What was the murder weapon, and who was the murderer? How do you know? (The solution to the mystery is at the end of this chapter.)

Discussing the Reading

activity

In small groups, talk about your answers to the following questions.

1. Did you enjoy the mystery story "The Critic in the Storm"? Why or why not?

2. Do you ever watch or read mystery stories? If so, where (for example, on television, at the movies, in magazines or books)?

3. Do you have a favorite mystery story? If so, why is it your favorite? Summarize the story briefly and simply.

PART three

Building Vocabulary

Learning Word Families

When you understand the meanings and uses of suffixes (word endings), you can better learn vocabulary systematically. In other words, you can study word families—groups of related words with the same stem, or main part, but different suffixes. In some dictionaries, these related words appear in the *same* word entry; in other dictionaries, related words appear in separate entries. Here are examples of word families from the dictionary entries below.

nouns	verbs	adjectives	adverbs
murder (thing) murderer (person)	murder	murderous	murderously
mystery mystification mysteriousness	mystify	mysterious	mysteriously

mur·der¹ /ˈmɜrdər/ *n* **1** [C;U] the crime of killing a human being unlawfully: *She was found guilty of murder.|Police are still looking for the murder weapon.* —compare MANSLAUGHTER **2** [U] *infml* a very difficult or tiring experience: *At last I repaired the clock, but it was murder getting the pieces back in.*

mur·der² *v* [T] **1** to kill unlawfully, and on purpose: *a murdered man* see KILL (USAGE) **2** to ruin (language, music, etc.) by using or performing it badly **—murderer** *n*
mur·der·ous /ˈmɜrdərəs/ *adj* of, like, or suggesting murder: *murderous intentions|a murderous expression on his face* **—murderously** *adv*

mys·te·ri·ous /mɪˈstɪəriʸəs/ *adj* not easily understood; full of mystery: *the mysterious disappearance of my brother|They're being very mysterious* (= not telling anyone) *about their vacation plans.* **—mysteriously** *adv* **—mysteriousness** *n* [U]

mys·ter·y /ˈmɪstəriʸ/ *n* **-ies 1** [C] something which cannot be explained or understood: *Her death is a mystery.* **1** [U] a strange secret nature or quality: *stories full of mystery*

mys·ti·fy /ˈmɪstəˌfaɪ/ *v* **-fied, -fying** [T] to make (someone) wonder; completely BEWILDER: *I'm completely mystified about what happened.* **—mystification** /ˌmɪstəfəˈkeʸʃən/ *n* [C;U]

Use the following dictionary entries to complete items 1 to 3 in the chart on page 116. How many related words do you already know? Fill in the rest of the chart and then check your guesses in your dictionary. (XXX indicates that no common word exists for this part of speech in this word family.) There may be more than one correct answer for some blanks.

nerve¹ /nɜrv/ *n* **1** [C] any of the threadlike parts of the body which form a system to carry feelings and messages to and from the brain **2** [U] strength or control of mind; courage: *a man of nerve|a test of nerve*

nerves /nɜrvz/ *n* [P] *infml* **1** a condition of great nervousness: *She gets nerves before every examination.* **2 get on someone's nerves** to make someone annoyed or bad-tempered: *That loud music is getting on my nerves.*

nerv·ous /ˈnɜrvəs/ *adj* **1** afraid; worried: *I always get nervous before a plane trip.|a nervous smile* **2** of or related to the NERVOUS SYSTEM of the body, or to the feelings: *a nervous disease* **—nervously** *adv* **—nervousness** *n* [U]

per·fect¹ /ˈpɜrfɪkt/ *adj* **1** of the very best possible kind, degree, or standard: *The weather during our vacation in California was perfect.|* (fig.) *a perfect crime* (= one in which the criminal is never discovered) **2** complete, with nothing missing, spoiled, etc.: *She's 75, but she still has a perfect set of teeth.*

per·fect² /pərˈfɛkt/ *v* [T] to make perfect: *She went to Italy to perfect her singing voice.*

per·fec·tion /pərˈfɛkʃən/ *n* [U] **1** the state or quality of being perfect: *The meat was cooked* **to perfection.**

per·fec·tion·ist /pərˈfɛkʃənɪst/ *n* sometimes *derog* a person who is not satisfied with anything other than PERFECTION (1): *It takes him hours to cook a simple meal because he's such a perfectionist.*

per·fect·ly /ˈpɜrfɪktliʸ/ *adv* **1** in a perfect way: *She speaks French perfectly.* **—opposite imperfectly 2** very; completely: *The walls must be perfectly clean before you paint them.*

sur·prise¹ /sərˈpraɪz, səˈpraɪz/ *n* **1** [U] the feeling caused by an unexpected event **2** [A;C] an unexpected event: *It was a pleasant surprise to see him again.|a surprise meeting*

sur·prise² *v* **-prised, -prising** [T] **1** to cause surprise to: *The taste surprised him; it was not as he had imagined it.|I was surprised to hear that his wife had left him.* **2** to come on or attack when unprepared: *They surprised us with a visit.*

sur·pris·ing /sərˈpraɪzɪŋ, səˈpraɪ-/ *adj* causing surprise: *It's not surprising that they lost the game.* **—surprisingly** *adv*

nouns	verbs	adjectives	adverbs
1. nerve(s) nervousness	XXX XXX	_____ XXX	XXX
2. perfection (thing) perfectionist (person)	_____ XXX	_____ XXX	_____ XXX
3. surprise	_____	_____ surprised	_____
4. critic	_____	_____	_____
5. _____	XXX	_____	possibly
6. fortune	XXX	_____	_____
7. _____	XXX	strange	_____
8. silence	_____	_____	_____

exercise 2   Complete the following story with words from the displayed words. For some blanks, more than one answer may be correct. The first few are done for you.

> murder   murderer   murderous
> mystery   mystify   mysteriously

In my favorite story, someone _____murder__ed a hotel manager. No one seemed to have a motive, so this ___murderous___ act _____mystif__ied everyone except the detective. _____ , she figured out the answer to the _____ quickly. The _____ was the chef.

> nerve   nervous   nervously
> perfection   perfectionist   perfect

The chef was a _____ —he insisted on _____ in the kitchen. Every meal had to be _____ . Because of the cook's perfectionism, the kitchen workers were always feeling _____ . One day the hotel manager had the _____ to talk to the cook about the problem. _____ , he went into the kitchen.

surprise   surprised   surprisingly
critic   criticism   criticize

The manager's _____ was a complete _____ to the chef. After all, no one ever _____d the cook because all the meals from his kitchen were perfect. Also, the manager was not a well-known food _____ . But _____ , the chef didn't get angry at the manager. Then the manager was _____ and worried.

possibility   possible   possibly
fortune   fortunate   fortunately

The next evening, the manager got a strange fortune cookie with his Chinese dinner. His _____ said, "You are _____ to get this warning about your _____ death. _____ , you will die tonight. But _____ , now you know about the _____ ."

stranger   strange   strangely
silencer   silence   silent

When a _____ came into the dining room, no one said anything; everyone was _____ _____ . Suddenly, a _____ thing happened. A shout broke the _____ . A kitchen helper yelled, "Help! The chef is shot!"

(This mystery story is *not* to be continued. . . .)

 **exercise 3**

From the reading selections in Chapters One to Six of this book, list ten words that are especially difficult or useful to you. Be sure to write the words in the correct boxes of this chart. Then use your dictionary to complete the chart with related words. (If no common word exists for a part of speech, write XXX in that box.)

nouns	verbs	adjectives	adverbs

 **exercise 4**

You can learn new words well by using them in your own speaking and writing. Write a story. Use as many of the words as you can from your chart in Exercise 3.

PART **four**
Scanning for Information

Emergency Instructions

The front part of most telephone directories contains instructions for emergencies. You may not understand all the words, but you can usually figure out the meaning from clues in the context and the pictures.

Look at the following section from the telephone book. Then read the questions on page 120. Find the information as fast as you can. Write the answers on the lines. The first student with the correct answers is the winner.

POISONING

The home is loaded with poisons: Cosmetics, Detergents, Bleaches, Cleaning Solutions, Glue, Lye, Paint, Turpentine, Kerosene, Gasoline and other petroleum products, Alcohol, Aspirin and other medications, and on and on.

1. **Small children are most often the victims of accidental poisoning. If a child has swallowed or is suspected to have swallowed any substance that might be poisonous, assume the worst — TAKE ACTION.**

2. **Call your Poison Control Center. If none is in your area, call your emergency medical rescue squad. Bring suspected item and container with you.**

3. **What you can do if the victim is unconscious:**

   A. Make sure patient is breathing. If not, tilt head back and perform mouth to mouth breathing. Do not give anything by mouth. Do not attempt to stimulate person. Call emergency rescue squad immediately.

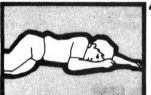

4. **If the victim is vomiting:**

   A. Roll him or her over onto the left side so that the person will not choke on what is brought up.

5. **Be prepared. Determine and verify your Poison Control Center and Fire Department Rescue Squad numbers and keep them near your telephone.**

Here are important words relating to emergencies:

poison = something that can kill people if they eat or drink it
swallow = to take through the mouth into the stomach
victim = the person who dies or is hurt
unconscious = not awake
vomit = to bring something up from the stomach through the mouth
roll = turn
choke = to be unable to breathe because something is in the throat

1. What are some examples of poisons? _____

   _____

2. Who are most often the victims of poisoning?_____

   _____

3. What are the two important words in step 1? What do they mean?

   _____

4. What is the first necessary action in case of poisoning?

   _____

5. What two places can you call for help in case of poisoning?

   _____

   In 6 to 9, complete the following sentences or answer the questions:

6. If the patient (victim) is unconscious, you need to find out if he or she is

   _____

   If not, you have to _____

   _____and

   _____

7. Can you give an unconscious victim water?_____

8. If the patient is vomiting, you should _____

   _____

   Why? _____

9. How can you be prepared for an emergency (poisoning)?

   _____

Going Beyond the Text

exercise **1**

Find the telephone numbers of the Poison Control Center and the Fire Department Rescue Squad in your local telephone directory. Then find other emergency phone numbers for your city or community. Write the numbers on the lines.

_____

_____

_____

_____

_____

exercise Work in groups. From the front pages of your local telephone directory, each student chooses the instructions for a *different* kind of emergency situation—for example, an earthquake, a fire, or a heart attack. Summarize the information. Then take turns sharing your information with your group and later with the whole class.

focus on testing

Antonyms

You already know the importance of synonyms when you are studying vocabulary. It is also helpful to learn antonyms. An antonym is a word with the opposite meaning of another word. For example, *seldom* and *often* are antonyms; they are opposite in meaning to each other.

Vocabulary tests often ask you to match words with their synonyms or antonyms. Read the directions carefully before you begin.

exercise Match the following words with their similar and opposite meanings. Write the correct letters on the lines. The first one is done for you.

SYNONYMS

1.	_e_ famous	**a.**	hurricane
2.	___ powerful	**b.**	lost
3.	___ cause	**c.**	strong
4.	___ murderer	**d.**	unfortunate
5.	___ storm	**e.**	well-known
6.	___ poor	**f.**	killer
7.	___ confused	**g.**	reason

ANTONYMS

1.	___ alive	**a.**	terrible
2.	___ happy	**b.**	sad
3.	___ loud	**c.**	calm
4.	___ upset	**d.**	poor
5.	___ wonderful	**e.**	stand
6.	___ rich	**f.**	dead
7.	___ lie down	**g.**	quiet

WHAT DO YOU THINK?

Here are descriptions of some strange events and experiences. Discuss your answers to these questions:

1. Which descriptions are real? Which are fiction? Why do you think so?
2. What do you think caused the real events and experiences? (Can you solve the real-life mysteries?)

(The answers are on page 126.)

1   **O**n a hot summer afternoon in 1794, there was a sudden heavy rainstorm in the village of Lalain, France. There were about 150 soldiers hiding in trenches (deep holes in the ground), and they had to come out. In the middle of the storm, little toads fell from the sky and jumped away in all directions. After the rain, the soldiers found many of the animals in their hats.

2   **O**n a farm in Tennessee on September 13, 1880, two children were playing in the yard. Their father came out of the house, talked to them, and started to walk across the field. Some relatives were riding by and were calling out to the man when he suddenly *disappeared from the earth*. There were no trees around and no hole in the ground. People looked for the man for a month, but they never found him. The grass at that place grew high because no animals wanted to eat it. A year later, the man's children and his wife heard his voice from the field. But the voice disappeared, and the man never came back.

Interactions I • Reading

3   **O**n December 5, 1945, a U.S. Air Force plane sent a message to the Naval Air Station at Fort Lauderdale, Florida: "This is an emergency. We cannot see land. We are not sure of any direction. We seem to be lost." Then the plane disappeared. In the morning, 21 ships and 300 other planes looked for the missing plane,  that, many planes and ships disappeared in the same area, called the Bermuda Triangle.

4   **O**n May 9, 1962, a tornado lifted a cow named Fawn from an Iowa farm. She "flew" about a half mile to a neighbor's field. Then she walked back home. Five years later, when the same thing happened, some tourists in a bus saw the "flying cow." After that, Fawn's owner always  put her in the barn when a storm was coming. Fawn died a natural death in 1978.

PART five
Personal Stories

Emergencies and Strange Experiences

The following three stories tell about an emergency situation and some unusual experiences.

Follow these steps for the stories.

1. Read each story quickly and tell the main ideas.
2. Answer your instructor's questions about the stories, and ask or answer questions of your own.
3. Give your opinions of the ideas in the stories.
4. Tell or write about an emergency situation or strange experience you have experienced.

1　　I live in California, and we have earthquakes here all the time. Sometimes they're strong. Things fall off shelves, and windows break. It's well known that a very big earthquake will probably hit this area in the near future. Everyone is preparing for it. Some people are terribly afraid. But usually we have small earthquakes. Sometimes we don't even notice them. For example, one evening I was sitting outside, on the patio. The ground began to shake very gently. At first, I wasn't sure it was an earthquake. It felt like I was in the water—in a swimming pool or a lake—with the water moving gently under me. I know this sounds crazy, but it was almost relaxing. I felt calm. Perhaps because of this experience, I'm not as worried about earthquakes as I used to be.

2　　Once, when I was a kid, I was on vacation with my father. We were driving to a national forest in the mountains. We had to cross a very hot, dry desert on our way to the mountains. Our car didn't have air conditioning, and the temperature was over 110 degrees. Every five or ten minutes I asked, "Are we almost there?" My father always said, "No. A few more hours." Then the most terrible thing happened. Our car broke down. It simply stopped there in the desert. We were a hundred miles from houses, gas stations, or people. We were hot, thirsty, and tired. I was very afraid. "We're going to die!" I said. (I was thinking of old movies on TV. People in old movies always die in the desert.) "We're not going to die," my father

124　　　　　　　　　　　　　　　　　　　　　　　　　　　Interactions I • Reading

said. "Yes, we are," I said. "There's nobody to help us. After two weeks the police will find our bodies, and. . ." Just then a car came by and stopped. "Need some help?" the driver asked. My father smiled at me. "You watch too much TV, kid," he said.

3   I often hear or read about "natural disasters"—the eruption of Mount St. Helens, a volcano in the state of Washington; Hurricane Andrew in Florida; the floods in the American Midwest; terrible earthquakes all over the world; huge fires; and so on and so on. But I'll never forget my first personal experience with the strangeness of nature—the "London Killer Fog" of 1952. It began on Thursday, December 4, when a high-pressure system (warm air) covered southern England. With the freezing-cold air below, a heavy fog formed. Pollution from factories, cars, and coal stoves mixed with the fog. The humidity was terribly high, and there was no breeze at all. Traffic (cars, trains, and boats) stopped. People couldn't see, and some walked onto the railroad tracks or into the river. It was hard to breathe, and many people got sick.

Finally on Tuesday, December 9, the winds came and the fog went away. But after that, even more people got sick. Many of them died.

All the events really happened. Possible explanations vary, of course: (1) Perhaps a whirlwind picked up the toads and dropped them to earth in a storm. (2) Maybe the man disappeared into the Fourth Dimension or an UFO (unidentified flying object) picked him up. (3) Maybe some places in the ocean can produce chemicals that take away people's sense of direction. Or perhaps the planes fell *up* into space into the Fourth Dimension. Or did UFOs pick them up? (4) Tornados sometimes pick up objects and put them down without damage.

Answers to the Descriptions of Strange Events and Experiences:

The murder weapon was the caviar, and Gregory Welles was the murderer. He had the caviar with him from his gourmet restaurant. There was no caviar in their hotel room when Althea Pennwright left her husband. Welles brought Ambrose poisoned caviar. He knew that Ambrose was reading a magazine because he saw him alive. (The magazine was not visible under Ambrose's large, dead body.) Also, Welles was lying when he said that he heard Ambrose's low voice from his hotel room because the wind outside was very loud. Ambrose loved food, so he ate all the caviar; then he died. Then Welles broke down the door and went to the hotel manager.

Answer to the Mystery "The Critic in the Storm":

CHAPTER seven

Health

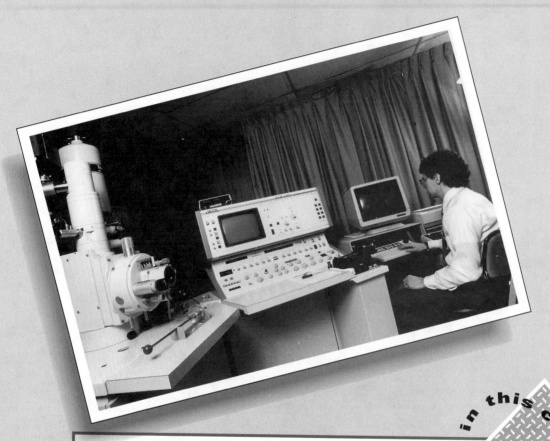

in this chapter

What age do you think of as "old?"
Seventy? Eighty? The first reading selection
is about some places of the world where
eighty-year-olds still have many years ahead
of them. In the second reading selection, you
will learn about some exciting technological
changes in modern medicine. Finally, you will
read about someone's experiences with
smoking.

PART ONE

The Secrets of a Very Long Life

Before You Read

Getting Started

Look at the picture and talk about it.

1. Where does it take place? Who are the two people? What are they doing?
2. Describe the lifestyle of the elderly couple. What do they probably do all day? What do they probably eat?
3. Do you know any very old people? How is their lifestyle similar to the lifestyle of the people in the picture? How is it different?

Preparing to Read

Think about the answers to these questions. The reading selection will answer them.

1. What places in the world are famous for people who live a very long time?
2. Describe the environment in these places.
3. What kind of diet do people in these places have?
4. What might be some secrets of long life?

Glancing at Vocabulary

Here are some vocabulary items from the first reading selection. You can learn them now or come back to them later.

NOUNS	ADJECTIVES	PHRASES
area	physical	not only . . . but also
secret	simple	health club
record	amazing	
eyesight	natural	
grain		
worry		

Read the following selection quickly. Then do the exercises after the reading.

The Secrets of a Very Long Life

A   There are several places in the world that are famous for people who live a very long time. These places are usually in mountainous areas, far away from modern cities. Doctors, scientists, and public health experts often travel to these regions to solve the mystery of a long, healthy life; the experts hope to bring to the modern world the secrets of longevity.

B   Hunza is high in the Himalayan Mountains of Asia. There, many people over one hundred years of age are still in good physical health. Men of ninety are new fathers, and women of fifty still have babies. What are the reasons for this good health? Scientists believe that the people of Hunza have these three benefits: (1) physical work, usually in the fields or with animals; (2) a healthful environment with clean air and water; and (3) a simple diet high in vitamins and nutrition but low in fat, cholesterol, sugar, and chemicals.

C   People in the Caucasus Mountains in Russia are also famous for their longevity. In this area, there are amazing examples of very long-lived people. Birth records are not usually available, but a woman called Tsurba probably lived until age 160; a man called Shirali probably lived until 168. His widow was 120 years old. In general, the people not only live a long time, but they also live *well*. They are almost never sick, and when they die, they have not only their own teeth but also a full head of hair, and good eyesight.

D   Vilcabamba, Ecuador, is another area famous for the longevity of its inhabitants. This region—like Hunza and the Caucasus—is also in high mountains, far away from cities. In Vilcabamba, too, there is very little serious disease. One reason for the good health of the people might be the clean, beautiful environment: The temperature is about 70° Fahrenheit all year long; the wind always comes from the same direction; and the region is rich in flowers, fruits, vegetables, and wildlife.

E In some ways, the diets of the inhabitants in the three regions are quite different. Hunzukuts eat mainly raw vegetables, fruit (especially apricots), and *chapatis*—a kind of pancake; they eat meat only a few times a year. The Caucasian diet consists mainly of milk, cheese, vegetables, fruit, and meat; most people there drink the local red wine daily. In Vilcabamba, people eat a small amount of meat each week, but the diet consists largely of grain, corn, beans, potatoes, and fruit.

F Experts found one surprising fact in the mountains of Ecuador: Most people there, even the very old, consume a lot of coffee, drink large amounts of alcohol, and smoke forty to sixty cigarettes daily!

G However, the diets are similar in two general ways: (1) the fruits and vegetables that the inhabitants of the three areas eat are all natural; that is, they contain no chemicals; and (2) the people consume fewer calories than people do in other parts of the world. A typical North American takes in an average of 3,300 calories every day; a typical inhabitant of these mountainous areas, between 1,700 and 2,000 calories.

H Inhabitants in the three regions have more in common than calories, natural food, their mountains, and their distance from modern cities. Because these people live in the countryside and are mostly farmers, their lives are physically hard. Thus, they do not need to go to health clubs because they get a lot of exercise in their daily work. In addition, although their lives are hard, the people do not seem to have the worries of city people. Their lives are quiet. Consequently, some experts believe that physical exercise and freedom from worry might be the two most important secrets of longevity.

After You Read

Getting the Main Ideas

Write T (true) or F (false) on the lines.

1. _____ Doctors and scientists study certain people to learn their secrets of long life.

2. _____ The areas of the world where people live a very long time are usually near the sea, and the weather is very hot.

3. _____ There is one main reason for the good health and long lives of these people.

4. _____ According to experts, most people in these regions eat mainly junk food, drink a lot of alcohol, and smoke cigarettes.

5. _____ The secrets of long life might be lots of rest and no hard work.

Guessing Meaning from Context

The questions after each of the following sentences will lead you to clues to the meaning of the underlined words. Find the answers and write them on the lines. Then circle the letter of the words that give the correct meaning of the underlined vocabulary items.

1. Doctors, scientists, and public health <u>experts</u> often travel to these places to study the causes of a long, healthy life.

   Who studies the reasons for a long, healthy life?_____

   _____

   Do doctors and scientists know about public health?_____

   Are doctors and scientists experts?_____

   What are *experts*? _____
   a. people who live a long time
   b. people who know a lot about a subject
   c. students
   d. travelers to many regions of the world

2. Scientists believe that the people of Hunza have the benefit of a healthful <u>environment</u> with clean air and water.

   What are two things that an environment can have?_____

   _____

   Where is the environment?_____

   What is an *environment?* _____
   a. clean air and water   c. a place in Hunza for scientists
   b. a healthful place   d. the conditions in a place that influence people

3. In this area, there are examples of very <u>long-lived</u> people. A woman called Tsurba, for instance, lived until age 160.

   Did Tsurba live a long time?_____

   What is Tsurba an example of?_____

   What does *long-lived* mean? _____
   a. having a long life   c. living in one place for years
   b. being 160 years old   d. being an example

 **exercise 3** Which words in each of the following sentences give clues to the meanings of the underlined words? Circle them. Then circle the letters of the words that give the correct meanings of the underlined vocabulary items.

1. People in the Caucasus Mountains in Russia are also famous for their longevity. In this <u>mountainous</u> area, the people not only live a long time, but they also live well.

longevity
a. long length of life
b. a long time
c. the environment of the mountains
d. health

mountainous
a. in the Caucasus
b. in Russia
c. having mountains
d. famous

2. Vilcabamba, Ecuador, is another area famous for the longevity of its <u>inhabitants</u>. One reason for the health of the people in this <u>region</u> might be the clean, beautiful environment.

inhabitants
a. the people of an area
b. cities
c. the environment
d. Ecuadorians

region
a. Ecuador
b. area
c. healthy place
d. beauty

Recognizing Reading Structure

Many reading selections follow an "outline." The outline is the plan of the material; it shows the relationship of the topics and ideas. The general parts of a main topic appear below it, and sometimes each part has details.

example: I. Reasons for Good Health of the Hunzukuts
      A. Physical work
         1. In the fields
         2. With animals
      B. A healthy environment
         1. Clean air
         2. Clean water
      C. A simple diet
         1. High in vitamins
         2. Low in fat
         3. Low in sugar
         4. Without chemicals

Interactions I • Reading

exercise 4   On the lines, answer the following questions about the sample outline above.

1. What is the one main topic of the outline? _____

2. How many general reasons are there for the good health of the people of
Hunza? _____What are the reasons? _____

_____

3. What two kinds of physical work do the Hunzukuts do? _____

_____

4. What are two characteristics of a healthy environment? _____

_____

5. How many characteristics of a simple diet are there in the outline? _____

exercise 5   On the lines, write the missing points in the following outline, according to the
reading selection. In the parentheses, write the letter of the paragraph that tells
about that topic.

I.   The secrets of a very long life

    A. Places where people live a long time

        1. Hunza (in the Himalayan Mountains)   ( )

        2. _____ ( )

        3. _____ ( )

    B. Diets of the three regions

        1. Differences   ( )

            a. _____

            b. Caucasion diet: milk, cheese, vegetables, fruit, meat, red wine

            c. _____

        2. Similarities   ( )

            a. Natural food

            b. _____

    C. Other causes of long life

        1. Hard physical work   ( )

        2. _____

Now circle the number of the one main idea of the reading.

1. There are several places in the world where people live a long time.

2. The secrets of longevity may be diet, physical activity, and freedom from worry.

3. In the Caucasus Mountains, people live even longer than people in Ecuador.

4. The inhabitants of mountain regions usually eat healthful foods.

Understanding Details

Punctuation often provides clues to the meaning of sentences and paragraphs. A colon (:) can introduce a list that explains the sentence before the colon. Sometimes each item of the list has a number before it. Commas separate the items. (If one or more items contain commas themselves, semicolons often separate the items.)

example: The elderly people of the area live well: (1) They are rarely sick; and (2) when they die, they have their own teeth, a full head of hair, and good eyesight. (What do the two numbered items show? Examples of how the elderly people live well.)

 Find the answer to each of the following questions about the reading selection. Write the answers on the lines.

1. According to scientists, what are the three reasons for the good health of the people of Hunza?

   a. _____

   b. _____

   c. _____

2. What are the characteristics of the environment in Vilcabamba, Ecuador?

   _____

   _____

3. How are the diets of the inhabitants of Hunza, the Caucasus, and Vilcabamba similar?_____

Sometimes a writer leaves words out of a sentence because the reader already knows them from other parts of the sentence.

example: The Hunzukuts eat mainly raw fruits and vegetables; the people of the Caucasus, mainly milk and meat. (The word *eat* is missing before *mainly milk and meat* because it appears in the first part of the sentence.)

 **exercise 8** Find the answer to each of the following questions in the reading selection. Write the answers on the lines.

1. How old were the two Caucasians in the reading (Tsurba and Shirali) when they died? _____

2. Between how many calories a day do the people of these three mountain regions consume?_____

 **exercise 9** Now turn back to the Preparing to Read section on page 128 and answer the questions.

Discussing the Reading

 **activity** In small groups, talk about your answers to the following questions.

1. How is your life similar to the lives of the people in these three regions? How is it different?

2. Are there any places in your country with groups of people famous for their longevity?

3. Think about some elderly people you know. Are they healthy? Do they have any "secrets" to long life? Can you suggest any other things that might lead to a long, healthy old age?

4. Do you hope to live a very long life? What will your lifestyle probably be if you live to be 100 years old?

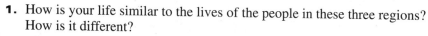

PART two

Disease Detectives

Before You Read

Glancing at Vocabulary

Here are some vocabulary items from the next reading selection. You can learn them now or come back to them later.

NOUNS	VERBS	ADJECTIVES	ADVERBS	PHRASE
medicine	determine	recent	moreover	birth defect
technology	detect	technological	previously	
transplant	cure	inherited		
organ	improve			
soil	fight (against)			
microscope	accept			
characteristic	raise			
organism				
bacteria				
virus				
illness				
knowledge				

Skimming for Main Ideas

 Read the following selection quickly. Then circle the number of the main idea of each paragraph.

Disease Detectives

Recent technological changes are making modern medicine a more popular and exciting field than ever before. First, new technology is now available to modern "disease detectives," doctors and scientists who are putting together clues to solve medical mysteries—that is, to find out the answers to questions of health and sickness. Second, knowledge of genetics may prevent or cure birth defects and genetic illnesses. Third, successful transplants of the heart, liver, kidney, and other organs of the body are much more common than they were ten or twenty years ago.

1. *Organ transplants are very common now.*
2. *Technological changes make modern medicine exciting.*
3. *Disease detectives can solve medical mysteries.*

B   Modern "disease detectives" include microbiologists, epidemiologists, and other scientists who try to find out the reason for an epidemic—a sickness that many people in one region have. These experts talk to people who have the disease and ask many questions, such as: What do you eat most often? How often do you wash your hands? Do you use drugs? They examine kitchens, bathrooms, and air-conditioning systems. Then they study the outside environment—soil, plants, rivers and lakes, areas for animals, and so on—for clues that might give them information about disease. They share the information that they find with laboratory scientists who have the benefits of microscopes and computers. Together, these disease detectives work to find the causes of modern killer diseases.

1. *Modern "disease detectives" are doctors.*
2. *Several kinds of scientists do many things to find out the causes of diseases.*
3. *Microbiologists study indoor and outdoor environments.*

C   What are genes and why are "disease detectives" always trying to find out more about them? Genes are part of the center (that is, the *nucleus*) of every cell; in the form of DNA (deoxyribonucleic acid), this "genetic material" determines the characteristics of every living thing—every plant, animal, and human being. Medical geneticists are scientists who study DNA and genes for many purposes: (1) to learn how organisms such as bacteria and viruses cause illnesses; (2) to detect the gene or combination of genes that causes inherited diseases like sickle-cell anemia, Huntington's disease, cystic fibrosis, and so on; (3) to understand the gene changes that lead to birth defects or genetic illnesses; (4) to change gene structure and thus prevent or cure genetic diseases; and (5) to improve the chances of success in organ transplants. For these and other reasons, genetics is an important part of modern science and medicine.

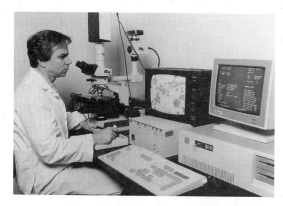

1. *Scientists study genetics for medical purposes, such as to cure birth defects and inherited diseases.*
2. *DNA consists of genes in the nucleus of every cell in every living organism.*
3. *Sickle cell anemia, Huntington's disease, and cystic fibrosis are genetic diseases.*

D   Organ transplants are more common today than ever before. Because of modern technology, moreover, they are more successful now than they were in the past: In other words, people with a new heart, liver, or kidney can live much longer than they used to previously. Not long ago, transplant patients often died after a few days because their bodies fought against the new organ. New drugs, however, now help the human body to accept a new part. In addition, knowledge of genes and DNA increases the possibility of successful organ transplants. As a result, doctors can try to "match" the characteristics of the organ donor (the person who gives the body part) and the receiver. In addition, scientists can change genes: Not only can they change the structure of DNA, but they can also put genes from one organism into another. In the future, therefore, scientists may put human genes into pigs or other animals, and farmers may raise animals for the purpose of organ transplants for humans.

1. *In the past, people did not live very long after transplants because their bodies didn't accept the new organs.*
2. *In the future, knowledge of genetics will bring people and animals closer together.*
3. *Because of modern medical technology, organ transplants are more common and more successful today than ever before.*

After You Read
Viewpoint

In many reading selections, the authors tell or imply (suggest) their opinions about the topic. What is the viewpoint of the author of the second reading selection in this chapter? Circle one of the choices in parentheses.

1. The author (believes / does not believe) in the use of modern technology to solve health problems.

2. She thinks that new developments in medicine are (good / bad) for people.

Work in small groups. Explain your answers to Exercise 1. Give reasons from the reading.

Learning to Summarize

If a reading selection or a paragraph follows a simple outline, you can summarize it easily. Just combine the important details with the main points in order, in as few sentences as possible.

For example, here are an outline and a summary of paragraph B of the reading selection "The Secrets of a Very Long Life."

OUTLINE	SUMMARY

I. Reasons for Hunzukuts' Longevity
  A. Physical work
    1. In the fields
    2. With animals
  B. A healthy environment
    1. Clean air
    2. Clean water
  C. A simple diet
    1. High in vitamins
    2. Low in fat
    3. Low in sugar
    4. Without chemicals
	There are several reasons for the longevity of the Hunzukuts of the Himalayan Mountains of Asia. First, they do a lot of physical work in the fields and with animals, in a healthy environment of clean air and clean water. Also, they eat a simple chemical-free diet high in vitamins but low in fat and sugar.

exercise 3

Work in groups of four. Each student chooses a different paragraph from the reading selection "Disease Detectives." Complete the corresponding outline forms A to D for your paragraph. Then summarize the information in a few sentences. Finally, take turns sharing your outline and summary with your group.

OUTLINE A   SUMMARY A

I.   Modern Medicine   _____

   A. New technology   _____

      1. Available to "disease detectives"   _____

      2. Trying to solve_____   _____

   B. Knowledge of _____   _____

      1. To prevent birth defects   _____

      2. _____   _____

   C. _____   _____

      1. _____   _____

      2. _____   _____

      3. Other organs

II. Finding Causes of Diseases   _____

    A. Kinds of "disease detectives"   _____

       1. _____   _____

       2. _____   _____

       3. Other scientists   _____

    B. What they do   _____

       1. Talk to people (ask questions)   _____

       2. Study the environment   _____

          a. Inside: kitchen, bathrooms,   _____
             etc.
                              _____

          b. _____   _____

       3. _____   _____

III. Genetics and Disease   _____

    A. What are _____?   _____

       1. Part of_____   _____

       2. Material that determines_____   _____

          _____   _____

          a. Plants   _____

          b. _____   _____

          c. _____   _____

    B. Purposes of the study of genetics   _____

       1. Learn how organisms cause   _____
          disease
                              _____

       2. _____   _____

       3. _____   _____

       4. _____   _____

       5. _____   _____

IV. Organ Transplants   _____

    A. Not so successful before   _____

        1. Patients died after a few days   _____

        2. Bodies fought _____   _____

    B. More common and successful   _____
       today

        1. _____   _____

        2. Knowledge of_____   _____

           a. Match_____   _____

              _____   _____

           b. Change_____   _____

              _____   _____

           c. Put_____   _____

              _____   _____

           d. Raise_____   _____

              _____   _____

Discussing the Reading

activity

In small groups, talk about your answers to the following questions.

1. What are some modern "epidemics" in your country, the United States and Canada, and the world? Do you know any of the reasons for these diseases? If so, share the information with your group.

2. Is it getting easier or harder to cure epidemics? Why?

3. What do you know about birth defects, genetic illnesses, and possible cures? Share your information.

4. What do you know about organ transplants? Do you think they are a good idea? Why or why not?

PART three

Building Vocabulary

Learning and Using Words with Prefixes

As you know, a prefix is a word element placed at the beginning of a root. Prefixes are like suffixes in that they change the meaning of the root and form a new word; however, prefixes do not change the word's part of speech.

Knowing the meaning of a prefix will give a clue to the meaning of the word. The following prefixes mean "no" or "not" and add negative meanings to words; that is, these prefixes create antonyms, or words with opposite meanings.

   dis-   il-   im-   in-   non-   un-

examples: The <u>discontented</u> expression on his face told us he was <u>unhappy</u>. (*Discontented* is the opposite of *content*; *unhappy* is the opposite of *happy*.)

You can often find a word with one of these negative prefixes in a separate dictionary entry (column 1) or within the dictionary entry for the main (opposite) word (column 2).

COLUMN 1

dis·sim·i·lar /dɪˈsɪmələr, dɪsˈsɪ-/ *adj* unlike; not SIMILAR.

il·le·gal /ɪˈliʸgə l/ *adj* [*no comp.*] not LEGAL; against the law: *It's illegal to park your car here.*–**illegally** *adv*

il·le·gal·i·ty /ˌɪliʸˈgælətiʸ/ *n* **-ties 1** [U] the state of being ILLEGAL **2** [C] an act against the law

im·per·fect¹ /ɪmˈpɜrfɪkt/ *adj* not perfect; faulty: *an imperfect knowledge of French* –**imperfectly** *adv* –**imperfection**

im·per·son·al /ɪmˈpɜrsənəl/ *adj* not showing personal feelings: *an impersonal letter* | *a large, impersonal organization* –**impersonally** *adv*

COLUMN 2

com·plete¹ /kəmˈpliʸt/ *adj* **1** having all necessary, usual, or wanted parts; lacking nothing: *John's birthday did not seem complete without his father there.* | *We bought a house* **complete with** *furniture.* –opposite **incomplete**

con·tent¹ /kənˈtɛnt/ *adj* [F+*to-v*/*with*] satisfied; happy: *Mary seems content to sit in front of the television all night.* –see also DISCONTENT

con·tent·ed /kənˈtɛntɪd/ *adj* [+*to-v*/*with*] satisfied; happy: *Jean seems contented just to sit and think.* –opposite **discontented** –**contentedly** *adv* –**contentment** *n* [U]: *the complete contentment of a well-fed baby*

142

non·ex·ist·ent /ˌnɑnɪgˈzɪstənt◂/ *adj* not existing: *This year's profits were very small; in fact, they were almost nonexistent.*

non·sense /ˈnɑnsɛns, -səns/ *n* [U] speech, writing, thinking, behavior, etc., that is stupid: *A lot of the government's new ideas are nonsense.* | *I've never heard such nonsense!* | *Stop that nonsense, children! Behave yourselves.* –see also SENSE¹ (3)

con·tin·ue /kənˈtɪnyuʷ/ *v* **-ued, -uing 1** [I;T +*to-v/v-ing*] to (cause to) go on happening: *The fighting continued for two days.* **2** [I;T +*to-v/v-ing*] to (cause to) start again after an interruption: *After a short break the play continued.* –see also DISCONTINUE

cor·rect¹ /kəˈrɛkt/ *adj* **1** right; without mistakes: *a correct answer* | *correct spelling* **2** keeping to proper standards of manners, etc.: *correct behavior* –opposite **incorrect** –**correctly** *adv* –**correctness** *n* [U]

for·tu·nate /ˈfɔrtʃənɪt/ *adj* –*more fml than* lucky– having or bringing good fortune; lucky: *He's fortunate in having a good job.* | *She's fortunate enough to have very good health.* | *It was fortunate for her that she had enough money to repair the car.* –opposite **unfortunate**

for·tu·nate·ly /ˈfɔrtʃənɪtliʸ/ *adv* by good chance; luckily: *I was late in getting to the station, but fortunately for me, the train was late too.* | *Fortunately, he found the money that he'd lost.* –opposite **unfortunately**

exercise 1

Which of these words contains a prefix with a negative meaning? Underline these prefixes. Put an X on the lines next to the words without a negative prefix. Use a dictionary if you need help. The first two are done as examples.

1. _____ incomplete
2. __X__ include
3. _____ important
4. _____ uncommon
5. _____ illegal
6. _____ inherited
7. _____ distance
8. _____ disagree

9. _____ nonstop
10. _____ impolite
11. _____ imply
12. _____ unfortunately
13. _____ impossible
14. _____ inhabitants
15. _____ illness
16. _____ uncomfortable

exercise 2 From the dictionary entries above and from your own knowledge, write the missing negative prefix (*dis-, il-, im-, in-, non-, un-*) in each blank. Then check your answers in the dictionary.

1. _____similar	**8.** _____sense	**15.** _____correct
2. _____appear	**9.** _____surprising	**16.** _____complete
3. _____balance	**10.** _____natural	**17.** _____honest
4. _____perfectly	**11.** _____popular	**18.** _____polite
5. _____active	**12.** _____mature	**19.** _____existent
6. _____ability	**13.** _____personal	**20.** _____successful
7. _____native	**14.** _____literate	**21.** _____ease

exercise 3 Look at the words in Exercise 2. Complete the following sentences about negative prefixes. Circle the correct answer.

1. Use _____ with most words that start with *b, m,* or *p.*
   a. *in-*
   b. *im-*
   c. *il-*

2. Use _____ with most words that start with *l.*
   a. *il-*
   b. *in-*
   c. *un-*

3. The most common negative prefix is _____ .
   a. *in-*
   b. *im-*
   c. *un-*

Reviewing Synonyms and Antonyms

You already know the importance of learning synonyms (or near-synonyms) and antonyms (or near-antonyms) when you study vocabulary. Not all words and expressions have antonyms, or opposites, of course; adjectives have opposites more often than other parts of speech.

exercise  Work in small groups. For each word on the left in the chart on the facing page, write a synonym (or near-synonym) and an antonym (or near-antonym). Use negative prefixes wherever possible. There may be more than one correct answer for some of the words. At the end of the chart, add five words of your own. The first group to correctly complete the chart is the winner.

	synonym or near-synonym	antonym or near-antonym
1. important		
2. pleasant		
3. healthy		
4. common		
5. fortunately		
6. exciting		
7. contented		
8. illegal		
9. noisy		
10. calmly		
11. increase (v)		
12. marry		
13. harm (v)		
14. advantages		
15. disease		
16.		
17.		
18.		
19.		
20.		

Recognizing Paraphrases

When you take a reading test, you often read a passage and then choose the sentence or sentences that best *paraphrases* the information in the passage, that is, says it another way.

example: Recent technological changes are making modern medicine a more popular and exciting field of study than ever before. (This sentence means: "Medicine is more exciting now than it used to be because of recent technological changes, so more people want to study it.")

exercise For each of the following items, circle the letter of the paraphrase (the sentence with a similar meaning).

1. Fortunately, new technology is now available to modern "disease detectives" who are putting together clues to solve medical mysteries.
   a. Modern science helps "disease detectives" answer the questions of medicine.
   b. We are fortunate to have technology in medicine.
   c. Detectives need new clues to solve the mysteries of sick people.

2. Transplants of the heart, liver, kidneys, and other organs of the body are much more common now than they were ten or twenty years ago.
   a. Transplants of body organs were not common ten years ago.
   b. The heart, the liver, and the kidneys are organs; doctors transplant them from one body to another much more often now than previously.
   c. People with organ transplants are much healthier than people who lived twenty years ago.

3. Because of modern technology, organ transplants are more successful today than they were in the past. Not long ago, transplant patients often died after a few days because their bodies fought against the new organ. A new drug, however, now helps the human body accept its new part.
   a. Organ transplants were not successful in the past because doctors did not give their patients drugs.
   b. Today, patients never die after an organ transplant because their bodies accept it.
   c. With a new drug, organ transplants succeed more often because the patient's body does not fight against the new organ.

PART four

Scanning for Information

Medicine Labels

 exercise 1   Here and on page 148, look at the labels from medicine packages. Then read the questions on pages 148 and 149. Find the information as fast as you can. Write the answers on the lines. The first student with the correct answers is the winner.

Here are some useful words from medicine labels:

> prescription = doctor's directions for medicine
> as directed = the way that the doctor said to take it
> capsule, tablet = kinds of pills
> discard = throw away
> dosage = amount that you should take
> exp. (or expir.) = expiration date (do not use the drug after this date)
> orally = by mouth
> internal = inside the body
> external = outside the body
> soothe = to make something feel better

Courtesy of Proctor & Gamble

Pepto-Bismol provides soothing relief for: heartburn, indigestion, nausea, upset stomach and diarrhea.

ADULTS 2 TABLETS • Children 9 to 12 years 1 TABLET • Children 6 to 9 years 2/3 TABLET • Children 3 to 6 years 1/3 TABLET • For children under 3 years, consult a physician. Chew or dissolve in mouth. Repeat every 1/2 to one hour as needed, to maximum of 8 doses in a 24-hour period. If symptoms persist consult a physician. Each 2 tablet dose is a full liquid dose in concentrated form.

Keep all medicines out of reach of children.

NO. 468492W DR MYERS

ONE TABLET DAILY WITH BANANA AND 1 GLASS OF ORANGE JUICE. DISCARD AFTER 6/97

FUROSEMIDE TABS 40MG SEARL 78498 26 MAY 96 KHN 10 EA

Courtesy of
Bristol-Myers Squibb Co.

THERAPEUTIC **MINERAL ICE®** PLUS MOISTURIZER is a fast acting, cooling pain reliever that brings you effective, penetrating relief while it covers your skin with a soothing moisturizer.
THERAPEUTIC **MINERAL ICE®** PLUS MOISTURIZER has a fresh scent, glides on smoothly, rubs in easily, soothes skin and penetrates deep to bring effective relief that lasts for hours.

For the temporary relief of minor aches and pains of muscles and joints associated with:
• Arthritis   • Strains, sprains, and bruises
• Simple backache   • Sports injuries

Adults and children 2 years of age and older: Clean skin of all other ointments, creams, sprays, or liniments. Apply to affected areas not more often than 3 to 4 times daily. May be used with wet or dry bandages or with ice packs. No protective cover needed. Children under 2 years of age: Consult a doctor. **USE ONLY AS DIRECTED. Read all warnings before use.**

KEEP OUT OF REACH OF CHILDREN. For external use only. Not for internal use. Avoid contact with eyes and mucous membranes. Do not use with other ointments, creams, sprays, or liniments. **DO NOT USE WITH HEATING PADS OR HEATING DEVICES.** If condition worsens, or if symptoms persist for more than 7 days, or clear up and occur again within a few days, discontinue use of this product and consult your doctor. Do not apply to wounds or damaged skin. Do not bandage tightly. If you have sensitive skin, consult a doctor **before** use. If skin irritation develops, discontinue use and consult your doctor. As with any drug, if you are pregnant or nursing a baby, seek the advice of a health professional before using this product. Keep cap tightly closed. Do not use, pour, spill or store near heat or open flame. **NOTE:** You can always use **MINERAL ICE®** PLUS MOISTURIZER as directed, but its use is never intended to replace your doctor's advice.

Menthol 4%.
Ammonium Hydroxide, Carbomer, Cupric Sulfate, FD&C Blue No. 1, Fragrance, Isopropyl Alcohol, Magnesium Sulfate, Petrolatum, Polysorbate 20, Sodium Hydroxide, Thymol, Water.
Store at room temperature.

DISTR. BY: BRISTOL-MYERS PRODUCTS
A BRISTOL-MYERS SQUIBB CO.
© 1992, New York, N.Y. 10154 MADE IN CANADA

CARTON MADE FROM 100% RECYCLED PAPERBOARD
MINIMUM 35% POST-CONSUMER CONTENT

Questions or comments? Call 1-800-468-7746.   TW7688-48-00

NEW
NDC 12843-161-53
Maximum

BAYER
ASPIRIN

Micro-Thin Coating
Caffeine Free

Fast Pain Relief of headaches,
muscular aches and pains, the
painful discomfort and fever
due to colds and flu.

30 TABLETS-500 MG (7.7 GRS.) EACH
153-03 A2

Maximum Bayer® Aspirin
Micro-thin Coating
Dosage: 2 tablets. Repeat after four
hours, if necessary. Do not exceed 8
tablets in 24 hour period.
Caution: If pain persists for more than 10
days, or redness is present, or in conditions affecting children under 12 years
of age, consult a physician immediately.
If pregnant or nursing, consult a physician before taking this or any medicine.
WARNING: Keep this and *all* medicines out of children's reach. In case
of accidental overdose, contact a physician immediately.

The Bayer Company, Glenbrook Laboratories
Div. of Sterling Drug Inc.
New York, N.Y. 10016
153W04 A3

Reprinted courtesy of The Bayer Company

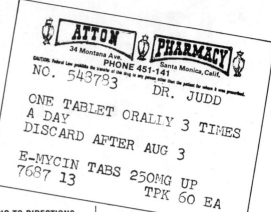

ATTON PHARMACY
34 Montana Ave.
PHONE 451-141
Santa Monica, Calif.
CAUTION: Federal Law prohibits the transfer of the drug to any person other than the patient for whom it was prescribed.
NO. 543783
DR. JUDD
ONE TABLET ORALLY 3 TIMES
A DAY
DISCARD AFTER AUG 3
E-MYCIN TABS 250MG UP
7687 13
TPK 60 EA

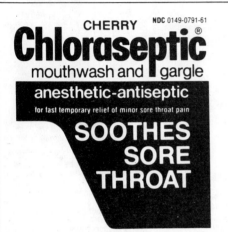

CHERRY
Chloraseptic®
mouthwash and gargle
anesthetic-antiseptic
for fast temporary relief of minor sore throat pain

SOOTHES
SORE
THROAT

LIST 79161
6 FL. OZ.
79161-L6

NDC 0149-0791-61

USE ACCORDING TO DIRECTIONS
As gargle, spray, or mouthwash

FOR PROMPT, TEMPORARY RELIEF OF DISCOM-
FORT OF MINOR THROAT IRRITATIONS AND
SORE THROAT DUE TO COLDS: Use full strength,
spray 5 times (children 6 to 12 years, spray 3
times) and swallow. Repeat every 2 hours if necessary. Or use full strength—gargle deeply following instructions in next paragraph.

FOR PROMPT, TEMPORARY RELIEF OF DISCOM-
FORT OF MINOR MOUTH AND GUM IRRITA-
TIONS: Use full strength, rinse affected area for 15
seconds, then expel remainder. Repeat every 2
hours if necessary.

FOR USE AS DAILY DEODORIZING MOUTHWASH
AND GARGLE: Spray full strength or dilute with
equal parts of water and rinse thoroughly, then
expel remainder. Chloraseptic removes mucous
secretions and fermenting food particles.

CAUTION: Severe or persistent sore throat or sore
throat accompanied by high fever, headache, nausea or vomiting may be serious. Consult your physician. If sore throat persists more than 2 days
consult physician. Do not administer to children
under 6 years unless directed by physician.
KEEP ALL MEDICINES OUT OF REACH
OF CHILDREN.

EXPIR. DATE   **Mar 95**

CONTROL

Courtesy of
Proctor & Gamble

1. Which four medicines can you buy in the drugstore without a prescription?

_____

2. What are the names of the prescription drugs? _____

_____

3. Which medicine is for a sore throat? _____

Which is for an upset stomach?_____

Which is for headaches and other pains? _____

4. Which medicine is only for external use? _____

5. How many Bayer aspirin tablets can a patient take at one time?_____

How often can the patient take aspirin? _____

6. How do people use Chloraseptic? _____

7. How much medicine is there in a bottle of Bayer aspirin? _____

_____

How much is there in a bottle of Chloraseptic? _____

_____

8. What is today's date? _____

Can a patient take E-Mycin today? _____

What is the expiration date of Furosemide? _____

9. Which label gives a toll-free (800) phone number to call if you have questions about the medicine? _____

10. What warning appears on most medicine labels? _____

_____

Going Beyond the Text

Bring to class magazine or newspaper ads about health (kinds of food, health products, brands of medicine, medical technology, and so on). For each ad, tell the class the following:

1. What product, service, or idea is the ad for?

2. What is the main idea of each ad? What health information does it give?

3. Can you use this product or service? Do you want it? Why or why not?

Bring some medicine containers to class. In small groups, take turns reading aloud the labels on some of the containers. The other group members guess what the medicine might be for.

In small groups, discuss your answers to these questions.

1. Do you or your family buy nonprescription drugs? If so, for what purposes? Do they help?

2. What health products or services do you believe in? In other words, what can you suggest to improve the health of your classmates or your instructor?

WHAT DO YOU THINK?

People often ask for health advice. They even write to health experts, who answer their questions in the newspaper. Are you an "expert" on health matters? Here are three situations of real people with health problems. Work in small groups. Discuss your answers to their questions.

1. My mother always has something wrong with her: a headache, a stomachache, a feeling of depression, and so on. She's always taking pills and tablets and capsules—sometimes she takes two or three prescription drugs at the same time. If she can't get a prescription for a refill from a doctor, she buys nonprescription pain killers from the drugstore. I know that it might be dangerous to take a lot of medicine, so I'm very worried about my mother. What do you advise?

2. I have a close friend; in fact, we grew up in the same neighborhood and went to school together. I just found out that he's HIV-positive. He's a great guy, and I don't want to lose him as a friend, but I don't know what to say to him. Also, when he gets AIDS, how can I spend time with him? I'll be so sad, and I won't know how to help him. And I may feel afraid for myself. The thought of AIDS makes me afraid. What do you think I should do?

3. I'm a college student, and I have to study a lot. I have to get good grades because if I don't, my father won't send me any more money for my education. My classes are very difficult, so I don't have time for recreation and fun. However, my real problem is my health: I feel tired and depressed most of the time. For these reasons, I can hardly concentrate on my studies. How can I solve this problem?

PART five
Personal Stories

A Dangerous Habit

The following story is about a woman's experience with smoking.

Follow these steps for the story:

1. Read it quickly and tell the main ideas.

2. Answer your instructor's questions about the story, or ask and answer questions of your own.

3. Make up an ending for the story. Explain why you think the story might end that way.

4. Tell your own opinions of the ideas in the story.

5. Tell or write about a health-related situation or problem of your own.

Up in Smoke

A   **I** began to smoke when I was in high school. In fact, I remember the evening I was at a girlfriend's house, and we were watching a movie—a terribly romantic movie. He (the hero of the movie) was in love, she (his lady) was beautiful, and they were both smoking. My friend had only two cigarettes from a pack in her mother's purse, and she gave one to me. It was my first time.

B   My parents didn't care much. They both smoked, and my older brother did too. My mother told me that smokers don't grow tall, but I was already 5´6″ (taller than most of the boys in my class), so I was happy to hear that "fact." In school, the teachers talked against smoking, but the cigarette advertisements were *so* exciting. The men in the ads were *so* good-looking and so successful, and the women were—well, they were beautiful and sophisticated.

C   I read a book called *How to Stop Smoking*. The writer said that smoking wastes time, and that cigarettes cost a lot of money. "So what?" I thought. The book didn't say that smoking can take away years of your life. But ten years later, everyone began to hear about the negative effects of cigarette smoke: lung disease, cancer, and heart problems. After that, there was a health warning on every pack of cigarettes. I didn't pay much attention to the reports and warnings. I felt healthy, and I thought I was taking good care of myself.

Chapter Seven • Health

D Then two events changed my mind. First, I started to cough. I thought it was just a cold, but it didn't get better. Second, my brother got lung cancer. He got sicker and sicker. My brother and I used to smoke cigarettes together over twenty years ago, and we smoked our last cigarettes together the day before he died. I sat with him in his hospital room, and I decided to quit. "No more cigarettes, ever," I said to myself.

E However, it was very hard to stop. Nicotine is a drug; as a result, cigarettes cause a powerful addiction. I tried several times to quit on my own—without success. I made excuses. I told myself: Smoking helps me keep my figure—i.e., I don't gain weight when I smoke. Smoking not only relaxes me but it also helps me think clearly. I'm a free, liberated woman. I can smoke when I want to.

F Finally, I ran out of excuses—I might say my excuses went up in smoke. I joined the "Stop Smoking" program at the local hospital. It still wasn't easy: For the first two months, I thought about cigarettes all the time. I didn't sleep well. I ate all the time, and I gained twenty-five pounds. I got very angry very quickly and easily—not only at important things but also at small ones. I was nervous, and my hands shook. Then. . . .

CHAPTER eight

Entertainment and the Media

in this chapter

Does TV turn people into "couch potatoes?" Are TV sets really "boob tubes"? Is TV responsible for the decline of the traditional family? The first reading looks at the positive and negative effects that TV has on us. The second reading is about a woman who confuses the fictional world she sees on TV with real life. Finally, you will read about three people's very different opinions of television.

PART one

Television: How It Affects Us

Before You Read

Getting Started

Look at the pictures below and talk about them.

1. What are the people doing?
2. How are the two groups of people different? How are their TV programs different?

Preparing to Read

Think about the answers to these questions. The reading selection will answer them.

1. In what ways might TV be beneficial?
2. What effects does TV have on the human brain?
3. How does TV cause us to be dissatisfied?
4. What effect does TV violence have on many people?
5. What are the signs of TV addiction?

Glancing at Vocabulary

Here are some vocabulary items from the first reading selection. You can learn them now or come back to them later.

NOUNS	VERBS	ADJECTIVES	PHRASES
the arts	affect	clear	as well as
brain	benefit	elderly	pay attention
		lazy	real life
			take a break

Read the following selection quickly. Then do the exercises after the reading.

Television: How It Affects Us

A   **H**ow does television affect our lives? It can be very helpful to people who carefully choose the shows that they watch. Television can increase our knowledge of the outside world; there are high-quality programs that help us understand many fields of study: science, medicine, the arts, and so on. Moreover, television benefits elderly people who can't often leave the house, as well as patients in hospitals. It also offers nonnative speakers the advantage of daily informal language practice; they can increase their vocabulary and practice listening.

B   On the other hand, there are several serious disadvantages to television. Of course, it provides us with a pleasant way to relax and spend our free time, but in some countries, people watch the "boob tube" for an average of six hours or more a day. Many children stare at a TV screen for more hours each day than they do anything else, including studying and sleeping. It's clear that the tube has a powerful influence on their lives and that its influence is often negative.

C   Recent studies show that after only thirty seconds of TV, a person's brain "relaxes" the same way it does just after the person falls asleep. Another effect of television on the human brain is that it seems to cause poor concentration. Children who view a lot of TV can often concentrate on a subject for only fifteen to twenty minutes; they can pay attention only for the amount of time between commercials!

D   Another disadvantage is that TV often causes people to become dissatisfied with their own lives. Real life does not seem as exciting to these people as the lives of actors on the screen. To many people, TV becomes more real than reality, and their own lives seem boring. Also, many people get upset or depressed when they can't solve problems in real life as quickly as TV actors seem to. On the screen, actors solve serious problems in a half-hour program or a thirty-second commercial.

E   Before a child is fourteen years old, he or she might view as many as eleven thousand murders on the tube. That child might begin to believe there is nothing strange about fights, killings, and other kinds of violence. Many studies show that people become more violent after certain programs. They may even do the things that they saw in a violent show. An example is the effect of "Beavis and Butt-Head," a cartoon show popular among teenagers in the early 1990s. After the program showed the title characters starting fires, several young people across the United States were responsible for setting fires. These fires caused serious injuries and property damage. In one case, a boy set the house on fire; his two-year-old sister died.

F   The most negative effect of the boob tube might be people's addiction to it. People often feel a strange and powerful need to watch TV even when they don't enjoy it. Addiction to a TV screen is similar to drug or alcohol dependence: People almost never believe they are addicted. Answer these questions about your TV habits:

1. *Do you come home from school or work and immediately turn on the TV set?*
2. *Do you watch more than ten hours of TV a week?*
3. *Can you concentrate for only fifteen to twenty minutes before you need to take a break?*
4. *Do you feel closer to actors on the screen than to real people in your own life?*
5. *Do you feel lazy and sleepy when you watch TV programs?*
6. *Do you believe that the products that you see on commercials can make you happier?*
7. *Are you dissatisfied with your life because it isn't exciting?*

If you answered "yes" to these questions, you probably have a TV addiction. The "cure" is to throw away the set.

After You Read
Getting the Main Ideas

exercise **1**   Write T (true) or F (false) on the lines.

1. _____ The effects of TV on our lives are always negative.
2. _____ Television affects the human brain.
3. _____ The lives of people who watch a lot of TV seem very exciting.
4. _____ Some people need to watch TV; they don't feel good without it.

Guessing Meaning from Context

Circle the words in each of the following sentences that give clues to the meaning of the underlined vocabulary item. Then circle the letter of the word that gives the correct meaning of the item. The first one is done as an example.

1. Television can increase our knowledge of the outside world; there are many high-quality programs that help us understand many fields of study: science, medicine, the arts, and so on.
   a. life   **b.** understanding   **c.** size

2. Children who view a lot of TV can often concentrate on a subject for only fifteen to twenty minutes; they can pay attention only for the amount of time between TV commercials!

   view   *concentrate*

   a. watch   **a.** enjoy
   b. enjoy   **b.** understand
   c. need   **c.** pay attention

3. To many people, TV becomes more real than reality, and their own lives seem boring because they are not as exciting as the lives of actors on TV.

   reality   *boring*

   a. real life   **a.** exciting
   b. programs   **b.** not interesting
   c. the present moment   **c.** worried

4. A child begins to believe there is nothing strange about fights, killings, and other kinds of violence.
   a. mysteries that detectives can't solve
   b. actions that hurt people physically
   c. arguments between people

5. The most negative effect of TV might be some people's strong addiction to it. They feel a strange and powerful need to watch it even when they don't enjoy it.
   a. enjoyment of   **b.** dislike of   **c.** need for

6. Addiction to TV is similar to drug or alcohol dependence: People almost never believe they are addicted. The "cure" is to throw away the TV set.

   addicted   *cure*

   a. intelligent   **a.** solution
   b. dependent   **b.** disease
   c. dissatisfied   **c.** reality

7. Do you believe that your life will be more exciting and happier if you buy the <u>products</u> that you see on TV <u>commercials</u>?

products	commercials
a. drugs or alcohol	**a.** exciting shows
b. things for sale	**b.** violent movies
c. benefits	**c.** advertisements

Recognizing Reading Structure

Circle the number of the *one* main idea of the reading.

1. Television teaches us about science, medicine, and the arts.
2. Television has several negative effects on people.
3. Television causes people to be violent.
4. Many people are addicted to TV.

> Sometimes a reading selection follows an outline. The outline shows the organization of the topics and ideas in the reading.

Put the following topics in the right places in the outline that follows. The letters in parentheses after the lines show the letters of the paragraphs that tell about the topics.

- The effect of TV on the brain
- The influence of TV violence on people
- The amount of time some people watch TV
- The positive effects of TV
- Television addiction, its signs, and its cure
- The comparison of TV programs to real life

TELEVISION: HOW IT AFFECTS US

I. _____ (A)

II. Disadvantages of TV

   A. The amount of time some people watch TV _____ (B)

   B. _____ (C)

   C. _____ (D)

   D. _____ (E)

   E. _____ (F)

Which of the details in items 1 to 13 on the facing page belong to which topics? In the parentheses, write Roman numeral I or the letters of the topics A to E from the outline in Exercise 4. Then turn back to the reading to check your answers.

1. (   ) A person's brain relaxes when he or she watches TV.
2. (   ) You can solve the problem of TV addiction if you throw away the set.
3. (   ) Some people watch TV for more than six hours a day.
4. (   ) Children aren't upset by violence because they see it all the time on TV.
5. (   ) Many people are addicted to TV.
6. (   ) Many children spend most of their time in front of the TV.
7. (   ) Television isn't good for concentration.
8. (   ) There are seven signs of TV addiction.
9. (   ) Some people do the violent things they see on TV.
10. (   ) Television offers high-quality programs on different subjects.
11. (   ) Nonnative speakers can improve their English by watching TV.
12. (   ) Because of exciting TV programs, some people become depressed or upset about their own lives.
13. (   ) Television helps people who can't move around a lot.

Understanding Details

 Circle the letters of *all* the correct phrases for each number and write the letters in the following blanks. For help, refer to the reading selection "Television: How It Affects Us."

1. Television _____ .
   a. can teach us about many subjects
   b. helps ESL students to learn English
   c. is better for children than for very old people
   d. increases our powers of concentration

2. Many people who watch a lot of TV _____ .
   a. cannot usually relax
   b. become dissatisfied with the reality of their own lives
   c. can solve their problems more quickly
   d. throw away their TV sets

3. Violence on TV _____ .
   a. may cause people to act violently
   b. is not very bad
   c. includes fights and murders
   d. affects only children

4. One "sign" of TV addiction is _____ .
   a. a set that you have on for more than one hour a day
   b. the need to turn on the set as soon as you come home
   c. a feeling of closeness to TV actors
   d. sleepiness when you see commercials but not movies

 Now turn back to the Preparing to Read section on page 154 and answer the questions.

Discussing the Reading

In small groups, talk about your answers to the following questions.

1. Do you have a TV set? How many hours do you watch it every day?

2. Which shows do you like most? Why?

3. Which shows don't you like? Why?

4. Does TV help you in any way? If so, how?

5. Go back to the reading (pages 155 to 156) and read about the signs of addiction again. Are you addicted to TV? If so, which signs of addiction do you have? Do you know anyone who is addicted to TV? Which signs does he or she have?

PART two

A Case Study

Before You Read

Glancing at Vocabulary

Here are some vocabulary items from the next reading selection. You can learn them now or come back to them later.

NOUNS		VERBS	CONJUNCTION	PHRASE
sofa	shampoo	reply	although	be in love with
symptom	jeans	hide		
boyfriend	trouble			
toothpaste				

Skimming for Main Ideas

Read the following selection as fast as you can.

A Case Study

A patient went into her doctor's office. She lay down on his sofa. The doctor sat in a large chair and opened his notebook.

"Oh, Dr. Brainstorm," she said sadly, "I'm so unhappy. What's wrong with me?"

"I don't know," he replied. "What are your symptoms?"

"Well," she began, "I'm not really sick, but I'm just so depressed all the time! My daily life is terribly boring. Although I do everything right, I'm not very popular, and I don't have any boyfriends."

"What do you mean, 'do everything right'?" asked the doctor.

"Oh, you know. I use Everwhite toothpaste and Perfect Shine shampoo. I wear Lovely Lady makeup and Extremely Slinky jeans. But nobody seems to like me. I can't understand it. I'm so confused!"

"Hmmm. I see," said Dr. Brainstorm. "What else is worrying you?"

"My life isn't the same as other people's. I think there something terribly wrong with me."

"What do other people do?"

"Well, Alicia, for example, is married to a successful microbiologist, but she's secretly in love with a computer expert whom she met at a health club. This computer expert, Max, still has a wife, a laboratory scientist, who is hiding on a mountainous island in the Caribbean because she killed a young man in a car accident four years ago. She's afraid that the police will find out and look for her. Alicia and Max don't know that the young man was actually Alicia's brother, a foreign student at a college in the Midwest."

"Amazing!" said Dr. Brainstorm. "How much time do you spend with these friends of yours?"

"Oh, about four hours a day."

"And how is your life different from theirs?"

"I just go to work, come home, watch TV, and go to bed. Nothing exciting ever happens to me."

"I see," said the doctor. "I think I know your trouble. You have a fairly common problem with reality. However, I know exactly how to solve it. Get rid of your TV set."

After You Read

Inferring: Figuring Out the Meaning

A reading selection gives information from which a reader can often infer, or figure out, other information. In this story, the writer only implies the main idea; that is, she leads the reader to the main idea, but she does not express it in words.

exercise 1 Look back at the reading selection "A Case Study" to find clues to the answers to the following questions. Write the answers on the lines. The answers will help you figure out the main idea.

1. Does Dr. Brainstorm try to cure patients' physical diseases or their personal problems?_____

How do you know this? _____

2. What does the patient do to be popular and find boyfriends? _____

_____

_____

3. In your opinion, where did the patient find out about Everwhite toothpaste, Extremely Slinky jeans, and so on? _____

4. In your opinion, who are the people that the patient discusses (Alicia, Max, and so on) in real life? _____

5. Reread the questions about TV habits on page 156. What are five clues to the patient's problem?_____

_____

6. What is the patient's problem? _____

7. How does the doctor want her to solve her problem?_____

_____

8. What is the main idea of this selection? _____

_____

Viewpoint

exercise 2 When a writer only suggests, or implies, the main idea of a reading selection—especially a story that is fiction—her or his *point of view* is probably implied too. What is the opinion of the author of the selection "A Case Study?" Circle one of the choices in parentheses.

The author probably thinks that TV offers (more / fewer) advantages than disadvantages.

exercise 3 Work in small groups. Explain your answer in Exercise 2. Give reasons from the reading.

Learning to Summarize

> To summarize a short fictional story, briefly tell what happened. Then tell the implied point (the "meaning") of the story.

 To summarize the story "A Case Study," complete the following paragraph.

A patient went to _____ because she

_____ . In answer to his questions, she explained

that although she _____ , she

was worried about two things. First, she _____

_____ .

Second, her life _____

_____ .

After he thought about her "symptoms," the doctor told her the solution to her

problem was to _____ .

The point of the story is that _____

_____ .

 Work in small groups. Take turns sharing your summary with your group. Are your paragraphs similar or very different? How?

Discussing the Reading

 In small groups, talk about your answers to the following questions.

1. The kind of program in which people such as Alicia and Max appear is called a "soap opera." Do you watch soap operas on TV? If so, which ones do you watch?

2. Tell the plot (story) of your favorite TV show.

3. What do you think about TV commercials? How are they good? How are they bad? How do they affect you?

4. What are your favorite commercials? Which commercials do you dislike? Why?

PART three

Building Vocabulary

Learning the Meanings of Word Parts

As you know, a suffix (word ending) often indicates the part of speech of a word. Like a prefix (word beginning), a suffix can also give clues to the meaning of the word. The stem (the main part of the word) has a meaning too. If you know the meanings of the word parts, you might be able to figure out the meaning of a new word. Here are the meanings of some prefixes, stems, and suffixes.

PREFIXES	MEANING
dis-	opposite; not
un-	not
re-	again
micro-	small
trans-	across
tele-	far

SUFFIXES	MEANING
-ology	the study of or the science of
-er *-ist*	a person who
-scope	an instrument (something) for seeing

STEMS	MEANING
bio	life
astro	star
port	carry; move

Sometimes you will see a word that you already know with a prefix or suffix. Here are two examples:

un | crowded
1. not   2. crowded

A definition of *uncrowded* is "not crowded."

nutrition | ist
2. nutrition   1. a person who

A definition of *nutritionist* is "a person who works in the field of nutrition."

exercise 1 Draw lines to divide each word into parts. Then write the meanings of the parts and the definition of each word.

DISSIMILAR

1. _____   2. _____

A definition of *dissimilar* is _____.

REINTRODUCE

2. _____   1. _____

A definition of *reintroduce* is _____.

exercise 2 Write the meanings of the parts of the following words. Then write the definition of each word.

ASTROLOGER

3. _____   2. _____   1. _____

Definition: _____.

MICROBIOLOGIST

3. _____   4. _____   2. _____   1. _____

Definition: _____.

exercise 3 Without a dictionary, match the words with their meanings. Write the correct letters on the lines. The first one is done as an example.

1. __C__ transatlantic
2. _____ epidemiologist
3. _____ unlimited
4. _____ microscope
5. _____ transport
6. _____ unintelligent
7. _____ epidemiology
8. _____ telescope
9. _____ microphotograph

a. not intelligent
b. something to help us see things far away
c. across the Atlantic Ocean
d. the study of epidemics
e. a small picture
f. not limited
g. to move something from one place to another
h. a person who studies epidemics
i. something to help us see small things

Using a Dictionary for Definitions and Examples

Some words have only one definition, or meaning. You can find the
definition in a dictionary entry, which sometimes includes an example.
(A definition is an explanation of the meaning of a word; an example
shows how to use the word in context.)

 Read the following two dictionary entries and answer the questions about them.
Write the answers on the lines.

microscope (5) [may´kr əskowp`], *n.* an instrument with a piece of special glass, or a combination of pieces of glass, that causes very small things to appear larger so that they become visible for study.

telescope (4) [tel´ əkowp`], *n.* an instrument for making distant objects seem closer and larger through the use of pieces of curved glass and mirrors. **Ex.** *He was studying the stars through a telescope.*

1. What part of speech is each word? _____

2. What is the dictionary definition of *microscope?* _____

_____

3. What is the definition of *telescope?* _____

_____

4. In a sentence, give an example of the use of the word *telescope.* _____

_____

Most words, however, have more than one meaning. Often the same
word can be more than one part of speech; each part of speech can have
a different meaning. Usually the various definitions of a word come in a
certain order in a dictionary entry: The most common meaning comes
first, the least common, last. *Note:* Every dictionary has its own style. The
entry below is from a different dictionary than the entries in Exercise 4.

example: [The word *opposite* is most commonly an adjective (adj); it
can also be a noun (n) or a preposition (prep). As an adjective,
it has two meanings (numbered 1 and 2 in this dictionary
entry).]

> **opposite** (2) [ap´əzit], *adj.* 1. against;
> exactly at the other extreme; differ-
> ent; contrary. **Ex.** *They held opposite
> ideas on the subject.* 2. facing each
> other; on the other side; on the other

end. **Ex.** *The two houses are on op-*
posite sides of the street. —*n.* that
which is opposite or very different.
Ex. *Happy people and sad people*
are opposites. —*prep.* facing. **Ex.** *We*
sat opposite each other across the
table.

 **exercise 5**   Read the above example. On the lines, write answers to the following questions.

1. What part of speech is the word *opposite* when it means "facing"?_____
Give an example of this use of the word in a sentence._____
_____

2. This entry gives four explanations of the first adjective meaning of
opposite. What are they?_____
_____

3. How many explanations does the entry give for the second adjective
meaning of the word? _____ For its noun meaning? _____

When you use a dictionary to improve your vocabulary, it is a good idea to fill in a "vocabulary chart." In the chart, you can list the same word (the same or different parts of speech) several times, each time for a different meaning. Be sure to copy (or create) an example that corresponds to each definition. For example:

word	part of speech	definition or synonym	example
1. opposite	adj	different; contrary	They held <u>opposite</u> views on the subject.
2. opposite	adj	facing each other	The two houses are on <u>opposite</u> sides of the street.
3. opposite	n	that which is opposite or very different	Happy people and sad people are <u>opposites</u>.

To complete the following chart, look back at the dictionary entries in Part Three of Chapters Four, Six, and Seven (pages 72, 115, and 142).

page number	word	part of speech	definition or synonym	example
72	1. direct	v	to tell the way to a place	Can you <u>direct</u> me to the station?
72	2. direct	adj	straight	
72	3. direction	n	control	
72	4. directly	adv	in a direct manner	
72	5. director	n	a person who directs a movie	
115	6. nervous	adj		I always get <u>nervous</u> before a plane trip.
115	7. perfect	v		She went to Italy to <u>perfect</u> her singing voice.
115	8. surprise	v		They <u>surprised</u> us with a visit.
142	9. continue	v		After a short break, the play <u>continued</u>.
142	10. nonsense	n		I've never heard such <u>nonsense</u>.

Make a chart like the one in Exercise 6. Then list ten words of your own from this book that are especially difficult or useful for you. Use a dictionary to find a definition and an example for each word in context. If there is no example, create your own.

Choosing the Correct Definition

As you know, many words in English have more than one meaning. For that reason, when you take a multiple-choice test, it is important to read each item very carefully. Tests will often try to "trick" you by including more than one synonym or definition of the underlined word among the possible answers.

example: Do you have any <u>free</u> time this weekend?
    a. not in prison
    b. costing nothing
    c. not busy
    d. empty

All four choices are definitions of the word *free,* but only one—(c) not busy—makes sense in this context

exercise   The following test items consist of very common English words with several different meanings. All the answers are synonyms or definitions of the underlined word in each item; however, only one answer has the same meaning as the word as it is used in the sentence. Circle the letter of the correct answer.

1. We <u>live</u> in Houston, Texas.
    a. are alive
    b. have our home
    c. continue to be
    d. can pay for what we need

2. A popular TV show tells the story of a couple <u>raising</u> a large foster family.
    a. lifting
    b. making larger
    c. producing
    d. taking care of

3. The average child in the United States <u>watches</u> 19,000 hours of TV by the end of high school.
    a. looks at
    b. looks for
    c. takes care of
    d. attends carefully to

4. Nobody can <u>see</u> why that talented actress is in such an awful TV show.
    a. find out
    b. understand
    c. make sure
    d. notice

PART four

Scanning for Information

TV Program Guides

exercise 1

You can see movies in many places—in movie theaters, on network and cable TV channels, and on videotape. You can also get information about these movies from many places—the entertainment sections of local newspapers, different kinds of TV guides, and so on. On the facing page, look at the page from the Los Angeles *Cable Guide*, a TV program guide. (Some of the abbreviations are explained in the box following the listings.) Then read the questions. Find the information as fast as you can. Write the answers on the lines.

1. Which movies are more than ten years old? _____
   _____

2. Which movies are relatively new (less than six years old)? _____
   _____

3. Which movie is the oldest? _____
   Which is a true story? _____

4. Which movies are about crime and the law? (These probably include violence.) _____
   _____

5. Which movies are about family relationships? How do you know?_____
   _____
   _____

6. Which movies start before noon (between 6:00 A.M. and 11:59 A.M.)?_____
   _____
   Which movies start after midnight (between 12:01 A.M. and 5:59 A.M.)?____
   _____

7. Which movies might interest children and teenagers? Why? _____
   _____
   _____

8. Which movies might interest you? Why? _____
   _____
   _____

170   Interactions I • Reading

Tatie Danielle (1991). Tsilla Chelton, Catherine Jacob. A mean-spirited elderly widow, who may or may not have caused her housekeeper's demise, moves to Paris to live with her grandnephew and turns his family's life into a living nightmare. (AT) Subtitled [PG-13, 1:52]: **BRV:** 25 (8p, 1x) ⩗

TC 2000 (1993). Billy Blanks, Bolo Yeung. When a dead cop is transformed into the ultimate killing machine, the former partner of the deceased lawman is called into action to stop it. R(V, AL) [1:36] **SHO:** 5 (11:05p), 10 (1:40x), 14 (12:35x) ☒

Teachers (1984). Nick Nolte, Judd Hirsch, JoBeth Williams. A disillusioned teacher is caught between the principal and an idealistic lawyer—one of his former students—when a lawsuit is brought against his high school. (AL, N) [2:00] **TBS:** 5 (10:05a)

Teamster Boss: The Jackie Presser Story (1992). Brian Dennehy, Jeff Daniels. This true story follows the dealings of the union leader who walked a dangerously thin line with ties to the mob, the FBI and top government officials. Made for cable. R(AL, V) [1:50] **HBO2:** 3 (11a, 9p), 18 (3p), 26 (11:30p), 29 (12n) ☒ ☻

Teen Angel. Jason Priestley, Adam Biesk. In order to gain admission to heaven, Buzz, a teenager who was killed in a 1950s car accident, must return to earth and perform a miracle for a modern teen. Part 1 [:30]: **DIS:** 7 (6p), 10 (1p) ☒ ; Part 2 [:30]: **DIS:** 14 (6p), 17 (1p) ☒ ; Part 3 [:30]: **DIS:** 21 (6p), 24 (1p) ☒ ; Part 4 [:30]: **DIS:** 28 (6p), 31 (1p) ☒

Teenage Mutant Ninja Turtles III (1993). Paige Turco, Elias Koteas. The shelled superheroes travel back in time to rescue their reporter pal after a magic scepter transports her to 17th-century Japan. PG(V) [1:40] **TMC:** 4 (7:25a, 5:10p), 13 (8:15a, 5:25x), 16 (8p), 21 (3:55p, 3x) ☒

Tell Me That You Love Me (1984). Barbara Williams, Nick Mancuso. A man feels slighted when he believes that his wife's career means more to her than their marriage. (AL) [2:00] **LIFE:** 14 (4p)

The Temp (1993). Timothy Hutton, Lara Flynn Boyle. A junior executive is about to get the axe—literally—when a psychotic stenographer with lofty career ambitions chooses to slay her way up the corporate ladder. R(V, ST, AL) [1:39] **HBO2:** 1 (1p), 10 (8a), 13 (8:45a), 21 (10p), 24 (6:15p, 4:05x), 27 (3:15p) ☒ ☻

Ten Tall Men (1951). Burt Lancaster, Jody Lawrance. A group of Legionnaires attempts to thwart an Arab invasion. [1:37] **MAX:** 7 (6:15a)

Tenor Titans (1991). Branford Marsalis hosts this look at the masters of the tenor saxophone, including John Coltrane, Zoot Sims and Coleman Hawkins. [1:00] **BRV:** 16 (5p, 11p)

Tentacles (1977). John Huston, Shelley Winters, Henry Fonda. When a giant octopus threatens to make a seaside community its lunch, killer whales come to the rescue. [2:00] **TBS:** 22 (11:50p)

The Tenth Month (1979). Carol Burnett, Keith Michell, Dina Merrill. A middle-aged divorcee becomes pregnant after a short-lived affair and chooses to raise the baby on her own. Made for TV. [1:58] **HBO:** 1 (9a), 14 (12:30p)

★ **The Terminator** (1984). Arnold Schwarzenegger, Linda Hamilton. A 21st-century android is sent back in time to murder the woman who holds a key to the future. Directed and co-written by James Cameron. (AL, V) [2:00] **USA:** 30 (8p), 31 (3p)

The Terror Within II (1991). Andrew Stevens, Stella Stevens. In a world ravaged by biological warfare, a warrior battles vicious mutants to save the remaining survivors from a deadly virus. R(N, GV, AL) [1:29] **HBO:** 5 (4:05x), 21 (2:50x)

Courtesy Cable Guide

Here are meanings of some of the abbreviations in the movie descriptions above.

Times:

a	=	6:00 A.M. to 11:59 P.M.
n	=	noon
p	=	12:01 P.M. to 11:59 A.M.
m	=	midnight
x	=	12:01 A.M. to 5:59 A.M.

Ratings:

AH	=	Adult Humor
AT	=	Adult Theme
AL	=	Adult Language
N	=	Nudity
R	=	Restricted
V	=	Violence
CC	=	Closed Captioned programs for the hearing impaired
E	=	Programs you can receive in Spanish *or* English
☆	=	a program of superior quality

Going Beyond the Text

Bring to class information about entertainment and the media, such as movie ads, descriptions of current movies (from the entertainment section of local newspapers), lists of currently available videotapes, local TV programs or schedules, and so on. In small groups or as a class, tell which programs or movies might interest you and why. Perhaps you can agree on a movie to attend together, a videotape to rent and watch in class, and/or a TV program to watch at home and discuss in class the following day.

PART five
Personal Stories

Television: Different Views

Follow these steps for the stories:

1. Read them quickly and tell the main ideas.

2. Answer your instructor's questions about the stories, or ask and answer questions of your own.

3. Tell your own opinions of the ideas in the stories.

4. Tell or write about your own opinions of television.

1   My television is an important piece of furniture to me. I can't get out of the house very often, but my TV brings the whole world to me. From the evening news and the "all-news" channels, I learn about events in the outside world: politics, the environment, recent changes in technology and medicine, and so on. I like game shows and travel programs, too. And I love comedies; I think it's important to be able to laugh. I can even watch shows in other languages and "go shopping" by TV. With the major national networks (CBS, NBC, ABC), the educational and cable channels, and the extra sports and movie channels, I have a choice of fifty different programs at the same time! Maybe I'll get a satellite dish. Then I'll have even more choices.

2   **O**ur son, Bobby, used to spend *hours* each day in front of the "boob tube." He was beginning to get strange ideas about reality from the violence and sex on many programs. Another problem was the commercials for children's toys. Bobby wanted everything he saw. Finally, we decided to have *no* TV. We put the TV set in the garage. Bobby was unhappy about this for a few weeks, but now he's learning more creative ways to spend his time: with friends, toys, books, and us!

3   **W**hen I came to this country, I didn't speak any English. I took classes and studied, but it wasn't enough. I wanted to learn faster. I began to watch TV for two hours every day: a half-hour of news, a half-hour comedy program, and a one-hour interview show where people asked and answered a lot of questions. I didn't understand anything at first. But then I discovered some new methods to help me understand: for instance, I watched the news in my native language first and then saw the same news in English. I also watched children's shows—the same show several times in the day; I understood almost *everything* in those programs. Sometimes I recorded a program on videotape and watched it again and again until I got the main ideas. Now I have a new idea: I can get closed-captioned TV for the hearing impaired and use it when I watch certain programs; then I can *read* the words in English subtitles at the same time I hear them. Now I think of TV as one of my best "teachers."

4   **T**elevision and the rest of the media confuse me. Sometimes I'm not sure what I saw on TV and what I experienced in "real life." I live in Los Angeles, where there are many TV and movie studios. Often in public places, I see people who look familiar to me. But did I meet them somewhere or did I see them on television? In addition, many "important" events in the news happen in my city. I can go to the event, or I can watch it happening on the screen. So many real happenings in the news—earthquakes and fires and murders and trials and so on—become "media events"; in other words, they grow "bigger than real life." After I watch them for many hours, I get confused. What is my life and what did the people in media create for me?

WHAT DO YOU THINK?

Here are the results of a survey of TV viewers in the United States. For each item, answer these questions:

1. Are you surprised by the answers? Why or why not?
2. Might people in your country answer the questions in the same or in a different way? Why?

1. *Question:* **How many hours of TV do you watch in a typical week?**

   Answers:

   Less than 7 hours 17%
   7 to 14 hours 29%
   15 to 28 hours 34%
   29 to 42 hours 13%
   43 to 70 hours 5%
   71 or more hours.....................1%

2. *Question:* **How many TV sets do you have in your home? Where are they?**

   Answers:

   2 or 3 sets 75%
   more than 3 sets 15%
   a set in the bedroom 55%
   a set in the children's room ..24%
   a set in the kitchen...............15%
   a set in the dining room 12%
   a set in the bathroom 3%

3. *Question:* **What else do you do while the TV set is on?**

   Answers:

   eat dinner 63%
   fall asleep 29%
   do other things 36%

4. *Question:* **What complaints do you have about TV?**

   Answers:

   too much violence 37%
   too much sex..........................27%
   too many commercials...........7%

5. *Question:* **Would you give up watching TV for the rest of your life for $25,000?**

   Answers:

   yes 23%
   no 77%

   Would you give up TV for $1,000,000?

   Answers:

   yes 25%
   no 75%

6. *Question:* **Suppose you have to live on a deserted island for one year. You can have only a telephone or a TV set. Which would you choose?**

   Answers:

   a telephone 61%
   a TV set 34%

CHAPTER nine

Social Life

in this chapter

The readings in this chapter have to do with friendship and other kinds of social relationships. The first two reading selections tell about some of the many ways young people meet possible husbands and wives. Finally, you will read different opinions of social life in the United States and Canada.

PART ONE

Meeting the Perfect Mate

Before You Read

Getting Started

Look at the picture story and tell about it.

1. Who are the people?
2. What are they talking about? How are the three people different from one another?
3. Do you agree with any one of them? Why or why not?
4. How do young people in your country often meet their boyfriends/ girlfriends?

Preparing to Read

Think about the answers to these questions. The reading selection will answer them.

1. What was a common kind of marriage in Korea in the past?
2. How do some Canadians and Americans meet the people who become their boyfriends or girlfriends?
3. What is an advantage to each method (way) of meeting people? What is a disadvantage?

Glancing at Vocabulary

Here are some vocabulary items from the first reading selection. You can learn them now or come back to them later.

NOUNS	VERB	ADJECTIVES	PHRASES
date	match	aggressive	arranged marriage
roommate		great	nightclub
guy		wonderful	dating service
wedding			

Read the following selection. Then do the exercises after the reading.

Meeting the Perfect Mate

For the past month I've been taking a graduate seminar called "Social Structure." It's a very popular course. We've been discussing friendship, marriage, and other relationships. One of our assignments is to examine the ways that people meet potential husbands and wives. I've been interviewing students on campus all week as part of my study.

First, I talked with my roommate in the dormitory, Sook In, a student from Korea.

"What's one way to meet a possible mate?" I asked her.

"Well," she said, "one method in my country is to have a matched marriage."

"A what?" I asked. "I know you can match a tie to a shirt—or two socks after you do the laundry. But people?"

"Sure," she replied. "There aren't many arranged marriages these days, but there were a lot not too long ago. My parents, for example, met each other for the first time on their wedding day. My grandparents chose their children's mates and arranged the wedding."

"Do you mean that they weren't in love? That sounds awful! Weren't they upset?"

"Maybe a little bit," Sook In said, "but they accepted each other. Then, fortunately, they grew to love each other. They've had a good, successful marriage for the past thirty years. This happens in a lot of arranged marriages."

I shook my head. "Amazing!" I said.

The next person that I interviewed was Bill, a guy in my business management class.

"I meet a lot of women in nightclubs—at least more than I do on campus," he said. "The environment is exciting and I go every weekend, if possible, to dance or talk or just listen to music."

"That seems great," I said.

"I thought so, too, at first," he said a little sadly. "But on the other hand, very often the women in those places are unfriendly. A lot of men are too aggressive, and as a result the women are very cold."

C

"Nightclubs? Never!" said Julie, a student who works part time in the campus bookstore. "I prefer to make new friends at places where people have interests in common. I met my boyfriend at the health club, for example, and it seems that the healthy atmosphere of the gym is continuing into the relationship that I have with him."

"That sounds wonderful," I said.

"Yes," she said, "I guess so. But to be honest, there's one problem with this arrangement."

"What?" I asked.

"The truth is that I really hate to exercise, so I don't want to go to the gym anymore. What's my boyfriend going to think when he finds this out?"

To be continued . . .

Getting the Main Ideas

 Write T (true) or F (false) on the lines.

1. _____ The writer of the selection has been interviewing students about ways to meet people socially.

2. _____ Arranged marriages were always unpopular in Korea because they were usually unpleasant.

3. _____ A nightclub is a wonderful place for everyone to meet friendly people.

4. _____ In some places, students can meet people who have common interests.

5. _____ The author of the selection has found a perfect way to meet new friends.

Guessing Meaning from Context

 Circle the words in the following sentences on the facing page that give clues to the meaning of the underlined word. Then circle the letter of the word that gives the correct meaning of the underlined vocabulary item. The first one is done as an example.

Interactions I • Reading

1. <u>Romance</u> should come naturally. A computer program can't lead to <u>true love.</u>
   a. nature
   b. love
   c. technology

2. We've been discussing friendship, marriage, and other <u>relationships</u>.
   a. problems
   b. people we like
   c. personal connections or associations

3. One of our assignments is to examine the ways that people meet <u>potential</u> husbands and wives. I've been interviewing students on campus. "What's one way to meet a possible <u>mate</u>?" I asked my roommate in the <u>dormitory</u>.

   potential   *mate*

   a. matched   a. friend
   b. possible in the future   b. marriage
   c. assigned   c. husband or wife

   dormitory

   a. classroom
   b. place for interviews
   c. place where students live on a campus

4. "Very often the women in nightclubs are unfriendly. A lot of men are too aggressive, so as a result the women act very <u>cold</u>."
   a. in need of a sweater
   b. sick
   c. not friendly

5. "I met my boyfriend at the health club, and it seems that the healthy atmosphere of the <u>gym</u> is continuing into the relationship that I have with him."
   a. nightclub
   b. restaurant
   c. place to exercise

Recognizing Reading Structure

 *exercise* **3**   Circle the number of the main idea of the reading.

1. People in nightclubs aren't friendly.

2. There are advantages and disadvantages to the various ways of meeting people.

3. Health clubs are good places to meet people.

4. Arranged marriages are usually successful.

**exercise 4**   The following outline shows the organization of the topics and ideas in the reading selection. First, on the numbered lines, arrange the following topics in order, as in the example. Look back at the reading if necessary.

- Arranged marriages
- Meeting people in nightclubs
- Meeting in health clubs
- Introduction: reasons for interviewing people

Then write the following ideas on the correct lettered line under each topic. The first one is done as an example.

- Mates may meet for the first time on their wedding day.
- You can talk or just listen to music.
- Husbands and wives may learn to love each other.
- The women act unfriendly because a lot of men are too aggressive.
- People with a common interest in exercise meet here.

I. _Introduction: reasons for interviewing people_ _____

II. _____

   A. _Mates may meet for the first time on their wedding day._ _____

   B. _____

III. _____

   A. _____

   B. _____

IV. _____

   A. _____

Understanding Details

> Often a writer leaves out words because information in other sentences or in another part of the sentence makes them unnecessary.
>
> *example:*   "What's one way to meet a possible husband or wife?" I asked.
>
>   "Well," she said, "one method in my country is to have a matched marriage." (Method for what? For meeting a possible husband or wife.)

 **exercise 5**

In the following sentences there are missing words that we understand. Which words are understood in these sentences? Write them in the blanks, as in the examples.

1. "Well," Sook In said, "one method _of meeting a possible mate_ in my country is to have a matched marriage."

2. "I know you can match a tie to a shirt—or _____ two socks, too, after you do the laundry. But _____ people?"

   "Sure," she replied. "There aren't many arranged marriages these days, but there were a lot _____ not too many years ago."

3. "Do you mean that they weren't in love? That sounds awful! Weren't they upset?"

   "Maybe _____ a little bit," Sook In said. "But they've had a successful marriage for thirty years."

4. "I meet a lot of women in nightclubs," Bill said. "At least more _____ than I do on campus. The nightclub environment is exciting. I go _____ every weekend."

Some words refer to ideas that came before them in the reading.

example: "My parents have had a good marriage for the past thirty years. This happens in a lot of arranged marriages." (What does *this* refer to? Having a good marriage.)

 **exercise 6**

In each of the following sentences, circle the words that the underlined word refers to. The first one is done as an example.

1. I've been taking a graduate seminar in Social Structure for the past month. It's a very popular course.

2. "One method is to have a matched marriage," Sook In said. "A what?" I asked.

3. "My grandparents chose their children's mates and arranged the wedding," she explained.

    "Do you mean they weren't in love?"

4. "I meet a lot of women in nightclubs—at least more than I do on campus."

5. "Nightclubs seem great," I said.

    "I thought so too at first," he said a little sadly.

6. "It seems that the healthy atmosphere in the gym is continuing into our relationship," she said.

    "That sounds wonderful," I said.

    "Yes," she said. "I guess so."

 **exercise 7**

Now turn back to the Preparing to Read section on page 176 and answer the questions.

Discussing the Reading

 **activity**

In small groups, talk about your answers to the following questions.

1. Do you know anyone who had an arranged marriage? Are there arranged marriages in your country? What is your opinion of this way to meet potential mates?

2. Have you ever gone to a health club or an exercise class? Did you enjoy it?

3. Where do people with common interests usually meet?

PART two

Meeting the Perfect Mate (continued)

Before You Read

Glancing at Vocabulary

Here are some vocabulary items from the next reading selection. You can learn them now or come back to them later.

NOUNS	VERBS	ADJECTIVES	PHRASES
date (person)	fill (out)	specific	make a mistake
height	miss	general	application form
feet (´)	film		no kidding
inches (˝)			produce section

Skimming for Main Ideas

Read the following selection quickly.

D

Meeting the Perfect Mate (continued)

"Computer dating services are the answer!" said my friend Sara, who lives down the hall from me in the dormitory. "They provide a great way to meet people! The biggest advantage is that you have a lot in common with the people you meet through a computer. The computer can match you up with someone of your same intelligence, astrological sign, age, lifestyle, and personality. For instance, you can meet someone who is creative, competitive, and honest, and you can ask for a scientist, an actor, a vegetarian, or . . ."

"Have you had many successful dates so far?" I asked.

"To tell the truth," she said, "no. I think I made a big mistake when I filled out the application form. I didn't want to miss a wonderful guy because of an answer that was too specific, so I was careful to write very general answers."

"What do you mean?"

"Well, there was a question about height. I said 'anyone between 3´5˝ and 7´5˝.' Then there was a question about recreation. I answered 'yes' to forty-seven interests, from gourmet cooking to camping in the wilderness.

I wrote that I liked swimming, hiking, the arts, comedy movies, quiz shows, mystery stories, business, ethnic foods, and so on, but I think that the computer got confused. It hasn't found a date for me since I sent in the application."

E

"And what about video dating?" asked Sara's roommate, Sandra.

"Dating by video?" I asked. "How is that possible?"

"Well, I haven't done it myself because it's expensive. But I've seen the ads on TV and in the newspaper. You join a video-dating club. They film you as you talk about yourself . . . you know, your background and your interests and things like that. Then you view videotapes of men, and if you want to meet someone, you write his membership number on a computer form. Then he sees *your* video, and if he likes what he sees on the screen . . . you arrange to meet!"

"Hmm. . . ," I answered. "More television in your life."

"Well, you could place a personal ad," Sandra continued.

"In the newspaper?"

"Sure. A friend of mine did that. He wanted to get married, so he figured out the statistics. He decided that out of every ten women, he liked one. And out of every ten women he liked, he might fall in love with one. Therefore, to get married, he just needed to meet one hundred women.

"Did it work?" I asked.

There was no answer.

F

Last I interviewed a guy in the cafeteria.

"Supermarkets," he told me.

"You're kidding," I said.

"No, I'm serious. I meet a lot of potential dates over the frozen pizzas in the convenience-food section. Also, it's easy to make small talk over the tomatoes and lettuce in the produce section. We discuss chemicals and nutrition and food prices. Sometimes this leads to a very romantic date."

I slowly shook my head: It is strange . . . very strange. I bit my lip because I didn't want to be impolite.

That evening, I talked with my roommate, Sook In.

"You know," I said. "I think maybe your parents and grandparents had a pretty good idea. A matched marriage is beginning to seem more and more practical to me."

After You Read
Inferring: Figuring Out Meaning

 exercise **1**

Often a reading selection gives information from which the reader can infer (figure out) other information. Write an X on the line in front of the ideas that the author stated (clearly said) or implied (suggested) in the reading selection. Write an O before the ideas that the writer did not state or imply. Look back at the reading selection if necessary. The first two are done as examples.

1. __X__ The writer's friend Sara is a student.

2. __O__ There is a computer dating service in the dormitory.

3. _____ Sara thinks that computer dating has many advantages.

4. _____ A computer application asks questions about height, interests, and other things, and the computer uses the information to match people for dates.

5. _____ Sara wants to have a date with a doctor who doesn't eat meat.

6. _____ Sara had much success with computer dating so far.

7. _____ If you join a video-dating club, you meet people on network TV.

8. _____ In video dating, two people can arrange to get together if they like each other's videotapes.

9. _____ To place a personal ad, you write about yourself and pay the newspaper to print the information.

10. _____ Dating and mating may be a matter of statistics.

11. _____ The student that the writer interviewed in the cafeteria likes computer dating services and video clubs too.

12. _____ He makes small talk with potential dates in stores.

13. _____ On dates, he likes to eat pizza with lettuce and tomato salad.

14. _____ The writer doesn't think that it is a good idea to date people you meet in the supermarket.

15. _____ The writer didn't tell her opinion to the guy in the cafeteria.

16. _____ She thinks that arranged marriages may have some advantages.

Learning to Summarize

The story in Parts One and Two of this chapter ("Meeting the Perfect Mate") is fiction, but it contains real information. One way to summarize the story is to tell the advantages and disadvantages of each possible way to meet people.

exercise **2**

Work in groups of six. Each student completes one of the following paragraphs. Then put your paragraphs together in a summary.

1. The writer has been interviewing people about friendship, marriage, and other relationships. She found out that the mates in arranged marriages

   _____

   _____ .

2. The advantages of meeting people at nightclubs are that _____

   _____

   _____ .

   The disadvantages are that _____

   _____ .

3. Some people make new friends at places where _____

   _____ , such as a gym. But there might be

   a problem if _____ .

4. An advantage of computer dating is that_____

   _____

   _____ .

   But if you _____ ,

   the computer might not _____

   _____ .

5. In a video-dating club, _____

   _____ .

   If you place a personal ad in a newspaper, you can meet _____

   _____ .

6. Some people think that the supermarket is a good place to meet potential

dates because _____

_____ .

But the writer thinks that _____

_____ .

Discussing the Reading

activity

In small groups, talk about your answers to the following questions.

1. Do you sometimes make small talk with people in places where you have interests in common? Do these people ever become your friends?

2. Do you have video and/or computer dating services in your country? What do you think of this way to find dates?

3. Where do you usually meet the people who become your friends? Where or how do you meet potential boyfriends or girlfriends?

PART three
Building Vocabulary

Distinguishing Between Adjectives Ending in *-ed* and *-ing*

As you know, sometimes you can tell what part of speech a word is from its suffix. The suffixes *-ed* and *-ing* both form adjectives when they are added to certain verbs. Adjectives ending in these two suffixes have very different meanings. Although they look alike, they are not synonyms or antonyms. It is important to be able to distinguish between adjectives ending in *-ed* and *-ing*.

An adjective with an *-ed* ending often describes a person or a person's feelings.

example: I get bored in nightclubs. (= Nightclubs bore me. I have a feel-ing of boredom when I go to them.)

An adjective with an *-ing* ending can describe a person or a thing: a cause of feelings.

examples: Nightclubs are boring. (= Nightclubs bore me. I feel bored in them.)

My date last night was boring. (= My date bored me. He wasn't interesting.)

exercise 1

Work with a partner. One partner explains the difference between the two sentences in item 1 and the other partner, the sentences in item 2. Follow the examples in the box on page 187.

1. **a.** That man is very irritating.
   b. That man is very irritated.
2. **a.** The people I meet at nightclubs aren't very interesting.
   b. The people I meet at nightclubs aren't very interested.

exercise 2

Complete the following paragraph with *interested, interesting, irritating,* and *irritated.*

Most of the students that the writer of "Meeting the Perfect Mate" inter-

viewed were _____ people. They were _____ in her

questions and wanted to help her with her survey. However, there were a few

who found her questions very _____ . They seemed

_____ by the questions and sometimes refused to answer at all.

exercise 3

Complete the following sentences with the correct form of the verb in parentheses.

1. (confuse) This map is very _____ . I am so _____ that
   I can't figure out which way to go.

2. (surprise) I was _____ when I ran into an old boyfriend at the
   supermarket yesterday. He told me some _____ stories about
   himself.

3. (excite) My parents will be _____ when they hear we're getting
   married. When should we give them the _____ news?

4. (bore) When she was in college, she went out with guys who were so
   _____ that she fell asleep on dates. Since she met her husband,
   she hasn't been _____ for a minute.

5. (amaze) They went to the _____ Grand Canyon for their honey-
   moon and were _____ by the natural beauty.

6. (tire) Many college students find the dating scene very _____ .
   They say they are _____ of trying to meet new people.

exercise 4   Work in pairs. Write ten sentences with *-ed* and *-ing* adjectives using the displayed verbs. The first pair with ten correct sentences is the winner.

amaze   embarrass   irritate
bore   excite   surprise
confuse   interest   tire

1. _____

2. _____

3. _____

4. _____

5. _____

6. _____

7. _____

8. _____

9. _____

10. _____

focus on testing

Easily Confused Words

There are several pairs or groups of words in English that you can easily confuse; that is, it is easy to mistake one word for another. These words often look and sound similar, but they are not synonyms. That means that you will misunderstand what you hear or read if you do not know how to tell these words apart. Reading and vocabulary tests will often ask you to show that you know the difference in meaning between these easily confused words.

example: disinterested/uninterested

    a. I'm totally <u>uninterested</u> in your argument, so please don't ask me to settle it.

    b. A(n) <u>disinterested</u> person should settle our argument.

Uninterested is the correct word for **a**; it means "not interested." The speaker is saying, "I don't care at all about your argument" or "Your argument doesn't interest me at all."

Disinterested is the answer to **b** because it means "willing to judge an act fairly because you are not influenced by personal advantage." Someone who is disinterested will not gain personally by deciding in favor of one side or another.

exercise Following are four groups of words that are often
confused and misused. Look at the definitions. Then
complete the sentences with the correct words.

1. accept/except
   Accept is a verb that means "to take or receive willingly"; "to
   believe," "admit," "agree to."
   Except is usually a preposition, meaning "leaving out," "not including." *Except* is also a verb, meaning "to leave out," "not include."

   a. Everyone has a date tonight _____ Tony.

   b. Sally has decided to _____ Lee's invitation to dinner
   and a movie.

   c. Sometimes small restaurants don't _____ credit cards.

2. allusion/delusion/illusion
   Allusion means "something said in an indirect way."
   Delusion means "a false belief."
   Illusion means "something seen wrongly, not as it really is."

   a. That poor young man is under the _____ that all the
   girls would love to go out with him.

   b. The professor's _____ to his students' love lives during
   his lecture was very funny.

   c. People often think they see water in the desert, but it is only

   a(n) _____ .

3. emigrate/immigrate
   Emigrate means "to leave one's country to go and live in another."
   Immigrate means "to come into a country to make one's home
   there."

   a. If you are going to _____ to the United States or
   Canada, it is a good idea to learn English.

   b. During the early 1900s, many people _____d from
   Europe to the United States and Canada

4. imply/infer
   Imply means "to suggest."
   Infer means "to draw the meaning from."

   a. I _____ from what you say that you don't want to go
   out with me anymore.

   b. Do you mean to _____ that you don't want to go out
   with me anymore?

PART four

Scanning for Information

Newspaper Ads for Social Activities

exercise ▸▸▸

Many college newspapers and some neighborhood newspapers have a section for news of social events. Look at the following announcements of social events. Then read the questions on page 192. Find the information as fast as you can. Write the answers on the lines.

1.
> TRAVELOG FILMS "Valley of Light" (Yosemite), "Simpatico Means Venezuela," "People of the Amazon" and "Assignment Yellowbird" (Florida and the Bahamas) are presented Saturday, October 15, 2:30 p.m. at the Santa Monica Public Library, 1343 Sixth St., Santa Monica. 451-5751.

2.
> POET ROBERT Mezey reads from his works Wednesday, October 19, 4-6 p.m. in CalArts Langley Hall. 805-255-1050.

3.
> SINGLE PARENTING—A one-day workshop for divorced single parents experiencing difficulties balancing the delicate and difficult act of being single and being a parent. Saturday, October 29, 9:30 a.m. to 4 p.m. at AID-WEST. Call Dr. Wilma Awerbuch at 824-0211 to register./

4.
> DR. ALAN H. Pressman discusses "Designing Your Diet" Friday, October 14, 7 p.m. at 845 N. Highland Ave. 871-2222.

5.
> "STARTING AND Managing Your Own Business" is offered Friday, October 14, 1-6 p.m. at USC. 743-2098.

6.
> BACH TO BLUES trio. Free concert Wednesday, October 19, 2 p.m. at Fairfax Library, 161 S. Gardner near Third.

7.
> "COPING WITH Stress: Basic Relaxation Methods" is discussed Wednesday, October 19, 7-8:30 p.m. at the Hollywood Presbyterian Medical Center, 1300 N. Vermont Ave. 660-3530, ext. 6350.

8.
> WANTED: FRIENDLY people to join me on all day sailing excursions, weekdays and weekends. No experience required, will teach. Leave message at 473-8550.

9.
> WEST VALLEY Jewish Singles, ages 18-28, attend Friday Night Services Friday, October 14, 8 p.m. at Temple Aliyah. Socializing and desert afterwards at a nearby coffee shop. Call Gregg, 703-0033, for details.

10.
> "WALKIN' SINGLES" takes semi-strenuous stroll through Marina del Rey Saturday, October 15, 1:30 p.m. meeting at 4754 Admiralty Way (in Boys Market parking lot). Historical narration. Age range 29-45 only. No smoking. Potluck picnic follows. To be included, phone 789-1035.

11.
> ROOKERY READINGS present poets Lance Jencks and Gerald Locklin, folksinger Michael Gleason and artist Debra Williams Tuesday, October 18, 8:30 p.m. at the Upstart Crow and Company, South Coast Village, Santa Ana. $2. 714-826-3094.

12.
> SAVE THE ANIMALS Fund is presenting The Animal Film, a comprehensive survey of the injustices committed against animals in the western society. Free showing Saturday, October 15, 12:30 p.m. at The Orange Room Cafeteria, Dept. of Water and Power, 111 N. Hope St. opposite the Music Center. Free parking Gate 6. 484-8766./

13.
> GAVIN DILLARD reads from his book "Notes From a Marriage. Love Poems" Sunday, October 16, 3 p.m. at A Different Light Bookstore, 4014 Santa Monica Blvd. 668-0629.

1. Match the social events in the newspaper section to the following interests. Write the numbers of the events on the lines.

   _____ animal life

   _____ travel around the world

   _____ classical and jazz music

   _____ being a better single (unmarried or divorced) parent

   _____ business

   _____ learning ways to relax

   _____ a healthy diet

   _____ social life for single Jewish people

   _____ poetry

   _____ sailing (traveling on a boat)

   _____ walking for health

2. Where might you meet people who share your interest in animals? _____

   _____

   What will you do in this place? _____

   How much do tickets cost to this event? _____

3. If you want to meet single people—and you like exercise and history—

   what phone number can you call for information? _____

   How old will the people at this event be? _____

   Can you smoke at this event? _____

4. When can you hear a concert of classical and jazz music? _____

   _____

5. Which event or events from page 191 interests you. Why? _____

   _____

Going Beyond the Text

Bring to class the "calendar" section of your newspaper or other articles with information about things to do and places to go in your city. List the new vocabulary items and find out their meanings. Read several items aloud and explain them to the class. Discuss the events and places. Choose one or more places to visit or events to attend. Make arrangements with one or more class-mates to go there. Then describe your experience to the class.

WHAT DO YOU THINK?

Proverbs are old, short, well-known sayings about human nature and life. Here are some popular English proverbs about friendships and relationships. First, match the proverbs on the left with their meanings (the paraphrases) on the right. Write the letters on the lines. Then for each proverb, discuss your answers to these questions:

1. Do you agree with the "wisdom" of the proverb? Why or why not? Give some examples from your own experience.
2. Is there a proverb with a similar meaning in your language? If so, translate it into English for the class and explain it.
3. Do you know any proverbs with an approximately opposite meaning (in English or in any language)? If so, tell about them.

1. _____ A friend in need is a friend indeed.
2. _____ One good turn deserves another.
3. _____ Familiarity breeds contempt.
4. _____ Live and let live.
5. _____ It takes one to know one.
6. _____ Two's company; three's a crowd.
7. _____ Love makes the world go around.
8. _____ Absence makes the heart grow fonder.
9. _____ All's fair in love and war.

a. If you don't see someone for a while, you will probably miss him or her.
b. Do what you want, and don't tell other people what to do.
c. You will always help a true friend.
d. If you know someone too well, you probably won't like her or him.
e. If you think someone is a certain kind of person, you may be that kind of person yourself.
f. If someone does a kind thing for you, you should do something kind for him or her.
g. In love relationships, as in war, anything is possible.
h. Love motivates people.
i. In love relationships, a third person just gets in the way.

Social Life in the United States

The following three stories—one in the form of a conversation—express different views of social life in the United States.

Follow these steps for the stories:

1. Read each story quickly and tell the main ideas.

2. Answer your instructor's questions about the stories, or ask and answer questions of your own.

3. Tell your own opinions of the ideas in the stories.

4. Tell or write about your own opinions of social life in this country.

1   **I** think I made a big mistake when I decided to come to this country. The educational system is okay, and in general it's a comfortable place to live, but life here can be very lonely. It's difficult to have close relationships with people here. Some Americans seem to hate foreigners. They're very cold to anyone different from them. Others are friendly at first, but they aren't really interested in a close friendship with a new person. And dating is impossible! I've dated several American women since I came here, but this hasn't been very successful. American women are too independent, too aggressive. Sometimes *they* suggest a place to go on a date. Sometimes they even want to pay for the dinner or movie. They don't understand romance.

2   **S**ome of the other students in my ESL class aren't very happy here in the United States because they don't have friends. I know it isn't easy, but they should try harder. I've been living here for a year and a half, and I've learned a lot about relationships with Americans. First, Americans who are interested in other cultures are friendly to foreign students. It's a good idea to spend time with such people; try folk dance clubs, international student groups, and so on. Second, it's important to be positive; don't tell a new American friend, "Your government is terrible. Americans are impolite. Your customs are wrong." Third, be open to new ideas. Customs aren't "right" or "wrong"—just different.

3
Sara:	Sook In! I haven't seen you in ages! How have you been?
Sook In:	Sara! I've been fine—just fine. And you?
Sara:	Great! So what's going on? I have so much to tell you!
Sook In:	Me, too! But when can we get together?
Sara:	Soon—very soon.
Sook In:	Why don't we meet for breakfast before class tomorrow?

Sara: Uh. . . that might be OK, but I don't have a class until noon, and. . . .

Sook In: Then how about in the afternoon? We could go to the gym together. . .

Sara: You know, I've never really liked to exercise. How about Saturday?

Sook In: Um . . . I work all day, but Saturday evening perhaps?

Sara: I have a date—a guy I met through the computer dating service.

Sook In: Well, let's get together soon.

Sara: Yes, soon. . . very soon.

Sook In: (*to herself*) Yeah . . . on February 30, maybe.

Sara: (*to herself*) Right . . . in July 2005.

CHAPTER ten

Customs, Celebrations, and Holidays

in this chapter

Do you know how to be a good guest at a dinner party? When you give a dinner party, do you know how to be a good host? The first reading selection gives some good advice on how to act in both those situations. In the second reading, you will learn about the history of a traditional holiday—Halloween. The final reading selection gives two very different views of Christmas.

PART one

Social Customs: A Dinner Party

Before You Read

Getting Started

Look at the picture and talk about it.

1. Where is the young man? What is he doing?
2. Why does he look confused? What is his problem?
3. What do you think he should do in this situation?
4. Have you ever had a problem like this? What did you do about it?

Preparing to Read

Think about the answers to these questions. The reading selection will answer them.

1. Who wrote the letters in the reading? Who answered them?
2. Should you bring something when you go to someone's house for dinner? If so, what?
3. At what time should you arrive for a dinner party?
4. What can you do if you don't know which knife, fork, or spoon to use at a formal dinner party?
5. If you give a dinner party, how can you help your guests feel comfortable?
6. What are some secrets of a successful dinner party?

Glancing at Vocabulary

Here are some vocabulary items from the first reading selection. You can learn them now or come back to them later.

NOUNS	VERBS	ADJECTIVES	PHRASES
invitation	arrive	late	make a mistake
kindness	thank	early	let someone know
card	act	shy	thank-you note
			spend time

Read the following selection quickly. Then do the exercises after the reading.

Social Customs: A Dinner Party

DEAR ETTY KIT

A **DEAR ETTY KIT:** My roommate's family wants me to celebrate Thanksgiving with them in their home. I accepted the invitation, and I'm excited about going, but I'm a little nervous about it, too. The social customs in my country are very different from here, so I'm a little worried about making mistakes.

Should I bring a gift, such as candy or flowers? Should I arrive on time or a little late? At the dinner table, how can I know which fork or knife to use? How can I let the family know that I'm thankful for their kindness?

CONFUSED

B **DEAR CONFUSED:** I suggest bringing a small gift when you go to a dinner party. Flowers are always nice, or you might bring a bottle of wine if you know that the family drinks it.

You should arrive on time or five to ten minutes late. Don't get there early. If you're going to be more than fifteen minutes late, I advise calling your hosts to tell them.

Try to relax at the dinner table. If you're confused about choosing the correct fork, knife, or spoon, just watch the other guests and follow them. If you still have no idea of what to do, don't be shy about asking the person next to you; it's better to ask than to be silently uncomfortable and nervous.

If you like the food, say so. Of course, you'll thank the host and hostess for the meal and for their kindness. It's also a good idea to send a card or thank-you note the day after.

C **DEAR MS. KIT:** I'm going to give a dinner party next month for some Canadian friends. I want my guests to enjoy themselves and to feel comfortable. What's the secret of giving a successful party?

WORRIED

D **DEAR WORRIED:** Cook something that let's you spend time with your guests. If a guest offers to help you in the kitchen, accept the offer. It often makes people feel more comfortable when they can help.

Before serving dinner, while your guests make small talk in the living room, offer them drinks. Those who drink alcohol might like liquor or wine, but make sure to provide soft drinks and fruit juice for people who don't. At the dinner table, let your guests serve themselves. Offer them a second serving after they finish, but don't ask more than once or twice. Most guests will take more if they want it.

Perhaps the most important rule of all is to be natural. Treat your guests as you want them to treat you when you're in their home—that is, act naturally toward them, and don't try *too* hard to be polite. Have a good time in a pleasant atmosphere.

News Press Syndicate

After You Read

Getting the Main Ideas

exercise 1 Write T (true), F (false), or I (impossible to know from the reading) on the lines.

1. _____ People write letters to Etty Kit, and she gives advice about social rules and customs.

2. _____ There are no social rules for dinner parties in the United States and Canada.

3. _____ Leaving a party on time is very important.

4. _____ When you give a party, you should spend all your time in the kitchen.

5. _____ Plan on making enough food for your guests to have two or three servings.

6. _____ It's important for both guests and hosts to feel comfortable; they should not try too hard to be polite.

7. _____ People in the United States and Canada have a lot of dinner parties.

Guessing Meaning from Context

exercise 2 Circle the words in each of the following sentences that give clues to the meaning of the underlined word. Then circle the letter of the answer. The first one is done as an example.

1. My roommate's (family) wants me to (celebrate) Thanksgiving with them in their home on (November 23). I accepted the (dinner) invitation, but I'm feeling a little nervous about it.
   a. a special day when families and friends have dinner together
   b. a thank-you note
   c. a celebration for roommates

2. Do you suggest bringing a gift such as candy or flowers?
   a. something to eat
   b. something to give another person
   c. plants

3. You should arrive on time or five to ten minutes late. Don't get there early.

   on time
   a. early
   b. not late
   c. at 8:00

   get there
   a. come to a place
   b. have something
   c. eat dinner

4. Don't be shy about asking; it's better to ask than to feel <u>uncomfortable</u> and nervous.
   a. comfortable
   b. loud
   c. not comfortable

5. After a dinner party, of course, you'll thank the <u>host and hostess</u> for the <u>meal</u> and for their kindness.

   host and hostess
   a. guests
   b. people who give a party
   c. cooks

   meal
   a. party
   b. gift
   c. dinner

6. Be sure to provide <u>soft drinks</u> and fruit juice for people who don't drink alcohol.
   a. juice
   b. fruit drinks
   c. drinks without alcohol

7. At the dinner table, let your guests <u>serve</u> themselves. Offer them a second <u>serving</u> after they finish.

   serve
   a. give food to
   b. talk to
   c. begin eating

   serving
   a. dessert
   b. conversation
   c. amount of food

Recognizing Reading Structure

 Circle the number of the main idea of the reading.

1. Always bring a nice gift when you go to a dinner party.
2. Just watch the guests at a party and follow them, and do not be shy about asking questions.
3. There are no secrets to giving a successful party.
4. If you follow a few simple rules for dinner parties, you can have a good time in a pleasant atmosphere.

 Following is the organization of topics in the reading selection. Write in the missing words; choose from the words *guest* or *host*. The first one is done as an example.

1. Letter from a _guest_____ who is going to a dinner party.

2. Answer to the _____ .

3. Letter from a _____ who is going to give a dinner party.

4. Answer to the _____ .

**exercise 5** The following ideas are from the reading. On the line next to each idea, write the letter of the section that the idea is from. The first one is done as an example.

1. __B__ It's a good idea to bring the host or hostess a gift.

2. _____ You should arrive at a party on time or a few minutes late.

3. _____ I'm nervous about going to a dinner party.

4. _____ I want my guests to enjoy themselves at a party that I'm going to give.

5. _____ Spend as much time with your guests as possible.

6. _____ When should I arrive at a dinner party?

7. _____ How do I choose the correct knife, fork, or spoon?

8. _____ Offer your guests drinks before dinner.

9. _____ How should I thank my host and hostess?

10. _____ Let your guests serve themselves at dinner.

11. _____ Watch the other guests at the table to find out what to do.

12. _____ Thank the host and hostess after the party and the next day.

Understanding Details

**exercise 6** In the blanks of the following sentences, write the words that are understood. The first one is done as an example.

1. My roommate's family wants me to celebrate Thanksgiving with them in their home. I accepted the invitation and I'm excited about going

   __to their home__ .

2. The social customs in my country are very different from _____ here.

3. If you still have no idea what to do at the dinner table, don't be shy about asking the person next to you _____ .

4. Of course, you'll thank the host and hostess for the meal. It's also a good idea to send a card or thank-you note the day after _____ .

5. Those who drink alcohol might like liquor or wine, but be sure to provide soft drinks and fruit juice for those who don't _____ .

6. Offer them a second serving after they finish _____ , but don't ask _____ more than once or twice. Most guests will take more _____ if they want it.

7. Perhaps the most important rule of all _____ is to act natural.

 In each of the following sentences, circle the words that the underlined word refers to.

1. I'm excited about going, but I'm a little nervous about <u>it</u>, too.

2. You might bring a bottle of wine if you know that the family drinks <u>it</u>.

3. If you're going to be more than fifteen minutes late, you should call and tell <u>them</u>.

4. If you like the food, say <u>so</u>.

 Now turn back to the Preparing to Read section on page 198 and answer the questions.

Discussing the Reading

 In small groups, talk about your answers to the following questions.

1. In your country, is it a good idea to arrive early, on time, or late for a dinner party? How late is "too late"?

2. Is it the custom in your country to bring a gift to the host or hostess? If so, what kind of gift?

3. Have you ever been to a dinner in a Canadian or American home? How was it similar to dinner parties in your country? How was it different?

4. Look at the picture at the beginning of the chapter. How is the table setting different from one in your country? What do you think each fork, knife, and spoon is used for?

5. In your country, do guests serve themselves or does the host or hostess serve them?

6. What is polite to do at a formal dinner party? What is not polite?

PART two

A Traditional Holiday

Before You Read

Glancing at Vocabulary

Here are some vocabulary items from the next reading selection. You can learn them now or come back to them later.

NOUNS	VERBS	ADJECTIVES	ADVERB	PHRASES
witch	hold	religious	unusually	hold on (to)
symbol	rule	holy		dress up
origin	frighten	magic		ring doorbells
festival		uneducated		"Trick or treat!"
god				
ghost				
spirit				
harvest				
goddess				
broomstick				
devil				
costume				

Skimming for Main Ideas

> Some writers give titles to each paragraph or section in a reading selection. The title of a paragraph or section should indicate the main topic.

exercise 1 Read the following four paragraphs quickly. Then put each of the following titles on the correct line. The first one is done as an example.

- Witches: A Symbol of Halloween
- The First Halloween
- Halloween Today
- The Origin of Halloween Customs

A Traditional Holiday

The First Halloween

Hundreds of years before the birth of Christ, the Celts—the inhabitants of parts of France and the British Isles—held a festival at the beginning of every winter for the Lord of the Dead. The Celts believed that this god ruled the world in winter, when he called together the ghosts of dead people. On October 31, people believed these spirits of the dead came back to earth in the forms of animals. They thought that very bad ghosts came back as black cats. At their festival on this day, the Celts used to make big fires to frighten the ghosts and chase them away. This celebration was the beginning of the holiday of Halloween.

B

The Romans, who ruled the British Isles after the birth of Christ, also held a celebration at the beginning of winter. Because this was harvest time, the Romans brought apples and nuts for the goddess of gardens. Later, the Christians added their customs to those of the Celts and the Romans. They had a religious holiday on November 1 for the saints (the unusually good people in Christianity), which they called All Hallows' or All Saints' Day. The evening before this day was All Hallows' Even ("holy evening"); later the name became Halloween.

C

Long ago in Britain, people used to go to wise old women called "witches" to learn about the future. They believed that these witches had

the power to tell the future and to use magic words to protect people or change them. There were many beliefs about witches, who are now a symbol of Halloween. For example, people believed witches flew on broomsticks to big, secret meetings, where they ate, sang, and danced. The Christians tried to stop people from believing in witches, but many uneducated people, especially in the countryside, held on to their beliefs.

D

When people came to North America from the British Isles, they brought their Halloween customs with them. Today, Halloween is a night when children dress up like ghosts, witches, devils, and so on. They go from house to house in their costumes, ring doorbells, and shout, "Trick or treat!" People give them candy, apples, gum, and nuts, and the children have a good time. But most children have no idea that their holiday has such a long history.

You can find out the main idea of a paragraph if you ask the questions "who," "what," "when," "where," "how," or "why" about the topic. By putting together the answers to these questions, you will get the main idea.

example: (paragraph A) Who celebrated? <u>the Celts</u> What? <u>a festival</u>
Why? <u>for the Lord of the Dead</u> When? <u>at the beginning of winter</u>
The main idea of this paragraph is that <u>the Celtic festival</u>
<u>at the beginning of winter for the Lord of the Dead was the</u>
<u>first Halloween.</u>

Answer the following questions about paragraphs B, C, and D. Then put together the answers to complete the main ideas.

PARAGRAPH B

1. Who celebrated the harvest? _____

2. Who celebrated All Saints' Day? _____

3. The main idea: The customs of _____

_____

PARAGRAPH C

1. What did people long ago in Britain believe in? _____

2. Why? _____

3. The main idea: _____ ,

a symbol of Halloween.

PARAGRAPH D

1. Who celebrates Halloween now? _____

2. How? _____

3. The main idea: Halloween today _____

_____

_____

Inferring: Figuring Out the Meaning

Write an X on the lines in front of the ideas that the author stated (clearly said) or implied (suggested) in the reading selection. Write an O before the ideas that the writer did not say or imply (even if the ideas are true). Look back at the reading if necessary. The first two are done as examples.

1. __X__ Halloween began a long time before the birth of Christ.

2. __O__ People today put candles in pumpkins (jack-o'-lanterns) to scare away ghosts.

3. _____ Ideas about ghosts, black cats, and witches are part of the celebration of Halloween.

4. _____ The early Romans were Christians.

5. _____ People associated apples and nuts with Halloween because they were symbols of the harvest in Roman times.

6. _____ One of the origins of Halloween was religious.

7. _____ The belief in witches came from Christianity.

8. _____ Witches could really fly and had the power of magic.

9. _____ Halloween customs came to the United States from Britain.

10. _____ The custom of trick-or-treating in costumes comes from the days of the Celts.

11. _____ If people do not give treats to children on Halloween, they might play tricks; thus, Halloween is a very dangerous holiday.

12. _____ People in many countries celebrate Halloween today.

Learning How to Summarize

In a summary, you should *paraphrase* the important information in as few words as possible. You can leave out the minor details and combine items into a series.

example: Some Halloween symbols are ghosts, black cats, jack-o'-lanterns, and witches.

You can combine short sentences with connecting words.

example: Because the Celts believed the Lord of the Dead called ghosts together on October 31, they made fires to scare away the ghosts.

exercise 4

Work in groups of four. Each student chooses a different paragraph from the reading selection "A Traditional Holiday." Summarize the information in your paragraph. Then take turns sharing your summary with your group.

Discussing the Reading

activity

In small groups, talk about your answers to the following questions.

1. Have you ever celebrated Halloween? If so, how did you celebrate it?

2. What two colors have you noticed at Halloween time? Can you guess what they mean?

3. Do you celebrate Halloween or a similar holiday in your culture?

4. Do some people in your culture believe in witches or in other people who can tell the future?

PART three

Building Vocabulary

Recognizing the Appropriate Definition

> As you know, most common words have more than one meaning. Often the same word can be more than one part of speech; each part of speech can have different meanings. When you use a dictionary to look up a word from a reading selection, it is important to choose the appropriate definition, that is, the meaning of the word as it appears in that specific context.

exercise 1

Read the following dictionary entries and answer the questions about them.

knife (2) [nayf′], *n.* a sharp blade for cutting, attached to a handle. —*v.* cut with a knife. **Ex.** *He was knifed in the back by the robber.*

witch (3) [wich], *n.* 1. a woman believed to practice evil magic. **Ex.** *The villagers thought a witch caused their trouble.* 2. an ugly old woman. **Ex.** *The old witch shouted at the children.*

1. How many parts of speech is the work *knife*?_____
The word *witch*?

2. Which definition (noun or verb) of *knife* means "an object on the dinner table"?_____

What is the other definition of the word?_____

208

Interactions I • Reading

3. Which definition (1 or 2) of *witch* is associated with the holiday of Hallow-

een? _____ Which is the other definition of the word? _____

_____

exercise 2

Read the following dictionary entries, paying close attention to the parts of speech, the different meanings, and the examples for each meaning. On the lines, write the part of speech and the appropriate meaning for the underlined word in each sentence. The first one is done as an example.

soft (1) [soft´], *adj.* 1. easily shaped, formed, etc.; yielding to the touch or pressure. **Ex.** *She likes to sleep on a soft bed.* 2. not strong, bright, sharp, etc. **Ex.** *A soft wind was blowing.* 3. gentle; tender; full of sympathy. **Ex.** *He spoke roughly to conceal his soft heart.* 4. smooth; delicate. **Ex.** *The baby's skin was very soft.* 5. quiet. **Ex.** *He spoke in a soft voice.* –**soft´en,** *v.* make or become soft. –**soft´ly,** *adv.* –**soft´ness,** *n.*

rule (1) [ruwl´], *n.* 1. an order; a guide for conduct which has been established. **Ex.** *Students must obey the school rules.* 2. the usual way of doing things; one's regular practice; usual behavior. **Ex.** *It is their rule to eat dinner late.* 3. the government of a king or other person in authority. **Ex.** *His rule over the country lasted*

thirty years. *v.* 1. govern; control. **Ex.** *The queen ruled her country well.* 2. decide officially. **Ex.** *The court ruled that their activities were punishable.* **rul´er,** *n.* a person who rules a country. **Ex.** *The country has had only three rulers during this century.* –**as a rule,** generally; most often. **Ex.** *As a rule, he will not go to meetings.* –**rule out,** eliminate from consideration. **Ex.** *He ruled out going back to school.*

shy (4) [šay´], *adj.* 1. easily frightened; or embarrassed. **Ex.** *She is a shy child.* 2. Short of a full amount or number. **Ex.** *We are a few dollars shy of our goal.*–*v.* draw back suddenly; start. **Ex.** *The horse shied at the approaching car.* –**shy´ly** *adv.* –**shy´ness,** *n.*

1. We served only <u>soft</u> drinks at our party because none of our friends drink alcohol.

adj. not strong. _____

2. The child had hard and <u>soft</u> candy in her Halloween bag.

_____

3. The weather was beautiful; there was a <u>soft</u> breeze blowing.

_____

4. You have to shout "Trick or treat!" Don't say it <u>softly</u>.

_____

5. The small child <u>shied</u> away from the big dog.

_____

6. The football team was only one point <u>shy</u> of victory.

_____

7. I'm too <u>shy</u> to wear a funny costume at a Halloween party.

_____

8. As a <u>rule</u>, children like holidays.

_____

9. Our front porch was a kind of social center; there were special <u>rules</u> for making small talk there.

_____

10. How long did people believe in the <u>rule</u> of the god of death?

_____

focus on testing

Making Analogies

Analogies are a common form of vocabulary question on standardized tests such as the TOEFL. Analogies are word relationships; they not only test your understanding of the meanings of words but also your ability to see the relationships among words and the ideas the words represent.

An analogy starts with two words in a specific relationship to each other—for example, *hot* and *cold*. A third word follows—for example, *wet*. Your job is to complete the analogy with a fourth word: a word that has the same relationship with *wet* as *cold* has with *hot*. The best answer here would be *dry* because *hot* and *cold* are opposites, and *dry* is the opposite of *wet*. In other words, you can say *hot is to cold as wet is to dry*. Or you can write hot : cold :: wet : dry.

Here are some examples (note that there is more than one correct answer for some analogies):

analogy	relationship between the words
festival : celebration :: lord : <u>god</u>	synonym
holiday : Halloween :: custom : <u>trick-or-treating</u>	an example or kind of
education : educated :: religion : <u>religious</u>	noun to adjective
February : March :: Saturday : <u>Sunday</u>	time sequence
gym : exercise :: supermarket : <u>shop</u>	place to do the activity

Interactions I • Reading

exercise 1 Complete each analogy with a word from the displayed words. Use each word only once.

appointment buy carrot dormitory day English foot host
bread kitchen last parent second see shoe store
temperature uncle

1. ear : hear :: eye : _____

2. head : hat :: foot : _____

3. drink : juice :: eat : _____

4. fingers : hand :: toes : _____

5. January : month :: Saturday : _____

6. mother : aunt :: father : _____

7. patients : hospital :: customers : _____

8. France : French :: Australia : _____

9. campsite : tent :: campus : _____

10. sail : boat :: cook : _____

11. saying : proverb :: date : _____

12. enemy : friend :: guest : _____

13. clock : time :: thermometer : _____

14. fruit : banana :: vegetable : _____

15. student : professor :: child : _____

16. hour : minute :: minute : _____

17. January : December :: first : _____

18. ask : answer :: sell : _____

exercise 2 Work in small groups. Explain your answers in Exercise 1, telling the relationship of each group of words (synonyms, antonyms, etc.). Then make up five analogies of your own. Exchange your analogies with another group and see if they can complete them.

PART four

Scanning for Information

Greeting Cards

exercise  Look at the following greeting cards. Then read the questions on page 214. Find the information as fast as you can. Write the answers on the lines. (In invitation 1, R.S.V.P. is the French abbreviation for Répondez s'il vous plaît, which means "please reply." B.Y.O.B. stands for "bring your own bottle," to indicate that you should bring whatever you want to drink.)

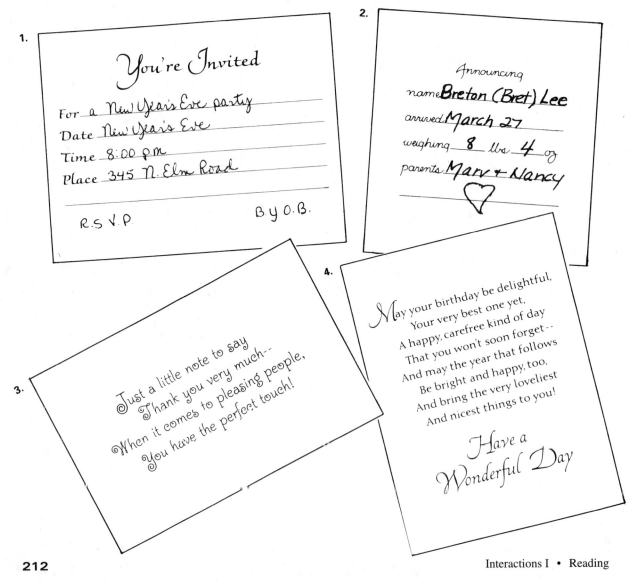

1.

You're Invited

For __a New Year's Eve party__
Date __New Year's Eve__
Time __8:00 pm__
Place __345 N. Elm Road__

R.S.V.P.   B.Y.O.B.

2.

Announcing
name **Breton (Bret) Lee**
arrived **March 27**
weighing __8__ lbs __4__ oz
parents **Marv + Nancy**

3.

*Just a little note to say
Thank you very much--
When it comes to pleasing people,
You have the perfect touch!*

4.

*May your birthday be delightful,
Your very best one yet,
A happy, carefree kind of day
That you won't soon forget--
And may the year that follows
Be bright and happy, too,
And bring the very loveliest
And nicest things to you!*

*Have a
Wonderful Day*

5.

Sorry to hear
of your hospital stay...
Hope you're improving
with every new day,
And before long you'll feel
well and happy again--
You'll be in my thoughts
and my wishes till then.

Hope You're Home Soon

6.

In times of sorrow,
when words of comfort
are needed most, it seems they are
most difficult to say.
May you find comfort
in the thoughts and sympathy
of friends.

7.

HOPE
HALLOWEEN
TREATS YOU
TO LOTS
OF FUN!

8.

As we greet the harvest season
in a joyful, grateful way,
Warm wishes go to your home
for a glad Thanksgiving Day,
And may the year that lies ahead
bring happiness and love
And all the special blessings
that you're so deserving of.

1. Which card is appropriate (correct) to send to someone on Halloween? Write its number: ____

2. Which card is appropriate to send to a widow? ____

3. Which card might you receive on your birthday? ____

4. Which card should you send to someone who is sick? ____

5. You went to a formal dinner party. You want to send a thank-you note to the hostess. Which do you send? ____

6. Which card might you receive on Thanksgiving? ____

7. A friend of yours recently had a baby. Which card did you receive? ____

8. Which card is an invitation to a party? _____ What time does this party begin? _____ How late (at least) does this party last? _____

   What two things should the guests do for this party? _____

   How do you know this? _____

9. Where should you send card 7? _____

10. Which card would you like to receive? _____

    Why? _____

Going Beyond the Text

Spend some time in the greeting card section of a drugstore or in a card shop at holiday time. Look at the different kinds of cards and other holiday items. If possible, copy some of the messages from cards. Discuss the experience with the class. What kinds of cards did you see? What were their purposes? What items did you see? What do people do with these things?

In small groups, take turns reading aloud some of the messages that you copied. Discuss new vocabulary. The other group members try to guess the occasion (purpose) of the card that the messages came from.

   What did you learn about North American holidays and customs from the cards? Discuss your ideas with the class.

PARTfive
Personal Stories

Christmas

The following two stories express two very different views of Christmas, the most important holiday of the year for many people in the United States and Canada.

exercise

Follow these steps for the stories:

1. Read them quickly and tell the main ideas.
2. Answer your instructor's questions about the stories, or ask and answer questions of your own.
3. Tell your own opinions of the ideas in the stories.
4. Tell or write about your own opinions of a holiday in the United States or Canada or in your country.

1   *E*very December, I begin to feel uncomfortable. Why? Christmas is coming. Most people enjoy this holiday, but it makes me depressed. First, I'm not a religious person. This holiday celebrates the birth of Christ, and it's full of religious symbols. Second, Christmas is becoming more and more commercial. It's the most important time of year for owners of stores, for example. Spending lots of money seems to be people's main activity in December. Everywhere you hear the commands "Buy! Spend! Give!" It's awful. Last, I think Christmas is a difficult time of year for people without families. I've been living away from my family for several years, and I miss being with them—especially at Christmas.

2   **C**hristmas is my favorite holiday. I enjoy baking Christmas cookies and planning parties. I like sending cards and hearing from old friends. I love seeing children open their gifts on Christmas morning. Most of all, I love one special custom that we have in our family. On the night before Christmas, we dress up in warm clothing and go from house to house in our neighborhood. At each house, we sing Christmas songs. Then we go to a hospital or a home for elderly people and we sing there. We want to let people know that we care about them. Afterward, we come home and drink hot chocolate by the fireplace. I love this!

WHAT DO YOU THINK?

Here are some descriptions of North American and international holidays and special occasions. For each description, discuss your answers to these questions:

1. What do you think the holiday or occasion is? (The answers are at the end of this chapter.)
2. Does your family celebrate this holiday? If so, tell the class about your customs.
3. If you don't celebrate the holiday or occasion, is there a comparable celebration in your culture? Explain.

1 **F**or Jewish people throughout the world, this fall holiday is the most serious day of the year. On this day, there's no eating or drinking. People go to the synagogue and pray. Then they can begin the new year with a clean heart.

2 **T**his historical holiday in the United States is the subject of political argument. On October 12, 1492, a European explorer arrived with three ships on an island in the Caribbean. Did he "discover America"? Or was he a conqueror and murderer of native peoples (the Indians)?

3   **I**n the year 1620, the ship *Mayflower* landed in New England, the northeastern region of the present United States. The Pilgrims, an English religious group, had a difficult first winter. But in spring they gave thanks for a successful harvest. In 1863, President Lincoln made the fourth Thursday in November a national holiday.

4   **P**eople throughout the world observe different customs on January 1, the first day of the year on the Western calendar. Some people clean their houses; some people attend special church services. In some places, there are fireworks. In the

United States and Canada, many people stay up late the night before to celebrate at parties. During the day, they visit friends and relatives and watch football games.

5   **O**n this very old holiday, Christians used to honor a saint on the day of his death, February 14. After eating and dancing, they played games to choose their mates. Now this is the day of "love and romance" in many places. People give cards, flowers, candy, and other gifts to their sweethearts.

Answers:

1. Yom Kippur   2. Columbus Day   3. Thanksgiving
4. New Year's Day   5. Valentine's Day

CHAPTER eleven

Science and Technology

in this chapter

Do you find the latest developments in science and technology exciting, or do some of the more dramatic advances frighten you? The first reading selection discusses how technology influences every aspect of our everyday lives. The second reading raises interesting questions about some controversial issues in technology today. Finally, you will read about the fascination— and the problems—one person has with modern technological equipment.

Everyday Uses of Technology

Before You Read

Getting Started

Look at the pictures and talk about them.

1. What area of science and technology might each picture or symbol represent— for example, atomic energy, chemistry, mechanics, etc.?
2. If you are an "expert" in one of these subject areas, tell the class a few facts about it.

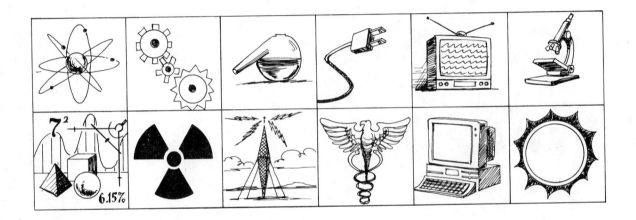

Preparing to Read

Think about the answers to these questions. The reading selection will answer them.

1. What are some controversial issues in science and technology today?
2. How can using a computer improve someone's social life and ability to communicate?
3. What are some examples of computer technology in the home?
4. What are some examples of advances in medical technology?

Glancing at Vocabulary

Here are some vocabulary items from the first reading selection. You can learn them now or come back to them later.

NOUNS	VERBS	ADJECTIVES	PHRASES
issue	create	controversial	carry on
aspect	last	electronic	get to know
contact	blame (for)		get around
rate	dial		break up
wavelength	collect		delivery time
appliance	distribute		in (large) part
privacy	pump		radio waves
	fit		genetically changed
	allow		high-tech
	instruct		radioactive tracer
	advance		interactive media
	attach		in the meantime
	slice		

Read the following selection quickly. Then do the exercises after the reading.

A

Everyday Uses of Technology

We often hear and read about controversial issues in science and technology. For example, will radiation from electronic equipment negatively change or destroy the environment? Can DNA testing solve a mystery by proving the guilt or innocence of a murder suspect? Should medical scientists change gene structure to prevent genetic disease or to create "more perfect" human beings? While people are arguing about these and other controversial subjects, technology continues to influence every aspect of everyday life—the home, health and education, entertainment and communication, etc.

B

Some people carry on active social lives with computers—their own or the ones available at terminals in public places like cafés, social centers, libraries, etc. Communicating with others on "bulletin boards," they get to know people they might never meet in traditional ways. For instance, a graduate student in San Francisco, California, has made more than fifty "net friends," including a homeless vegetarian who gets around on rollerblades, an HIV-positive police officer, some members of an Iranian family, an 80-year-old detective, and a medical geneticist who studies DNA. She has gone out on dates with about ten of her "network contacts." In fact, she almost married one. The romance didn't last, however; nevertheless, she doesn't blame the computer for breaking up the relationship.

C With modern telephone technology, many people stopped writing letters. But now, writing to communicate has been coming back in electronic form, or e-mail, which is a way of sending messages from one computer to another. When a computer is ready to "mail a letter," it dials a server—i.e., a central computer that collects and distributes electronic information. Delivery time from the sender to the receiver is no more than a few seconds, even from one country to another. For some computer users, the wish to communicate intelligently with others makes them want to write better. Here is a typical e-mail love letter:

> What you are to me is an emotional laser, matter into which I can pump light of any rate and wavelength.

D Computer technology has also helped make running a home easier. Many families have a microcomputer (a computer that fits on a table or desk) in their homes, which they use for everything from keeping household records and writing letters to playing computer games. In addition, many modern machines (e.g., entertainment equipment, kitchen appliances) contain computer chips that allow their owners to program them. For instance, you can "tell" a VCR (i.e., a videocassette recorder) which programs to record and when. You can "instruct" a microwave oven as to how to cook a certain dish. You can program your electric or gas range, dishwasher, washing machine and dryer, etc., to "do the housework" on their own.

E Largely because of the computer, technology continues to advance in the medical sciences. One example is the use of computer information in an ambulance before a patient even gets to the hospital. Emergency medical technicians can attach small sensors (i.e., devices with cables) to the patient (e.g., a heart attack victim) to get information about electrical activity in the heart and the brain. By radio and computer, they can send the information to the hospital so that medical specialists can get ready for the patient's arrival. In the meantine, technicians can get advice on how to keep the patient alive. Later, doctors can look into the patient's body in new ways—not only with X-rays but with CAT (computerized axial tomography) scans and DSA (dynamic spatial reconstruction) scans that photographically "slice through" an organ from any or many different views. Other methods of collecting medical information are based on sound (sonography), temperature (thermography), radio waves, radioactive tracers, and so on.

F   Although much of the technology in our everyday lives has only positive effects, there are some uses that raise controversial issues and questions. For example, are interactive media (i.e., a combination of television, telephone, and computer) going to control minds, destroy privacy, and cause people to forget about family life and personal relationships? What effects will genetically changed foods (e.g., fruits and vegetables created in a laboratory) have on people's health? High-tech medical treatments (organ transplants, changing gene structure, etc.) can increase the longevity of individuals, but can they improve the health and happiness of human beings in general? Only time will tell, but in the meantime, science and technology will continue to move forward.

After You Read
Getting the Main Ideas

 Write T (true), F (false), or I (impossible to know from the reading) on the lines.

1. _____ Because electronic machines are destroying the environment, science and technology cannot progress.

2. _____ These days, you need a computer in your home if you want to meet people, make friends, and get married.

3. _____ Instead of always using the telephone to communicate, some people are sending letters through "e-mail."

4. _____ With a microcomputer, you can program any TV set, VCR, oven, washer, and drier.

5. _____ Modern medical technology can prevent disease, but it can't help save or extend lives.

6. _____ The worst problem caused by modern technology is computer crime.

Guessing Meaning from Context

If a word or phrase has a new or special meaning in a specific context, it may be in quotation marks (" ").

example: When a computer is ready to "mail a letter," it dials a server. (What does "mail a letter" mean? The quotation marks show that in this special context, the phrase means that the computer is going to send a message electronically.)

Sometimes common, everyday words take on new or special (more "modern") meanings. In a small or old dictionary, you may not find the exact definition you need, but you can often figure out the meaning from the "modern" context.

example: Are there computer terminals at the bus terminal? (A bus terminal is a starting and ending point for buses. A computer terminal, then, must be a starting and ending point for electronic information.)

exercise 2 From the definition of the everyday words or phrases in *italics,* try to figure out the meaning of the underlined items in their new or special contexts. Then answer the questions. To find the item in context, you can look back at the reading selection. You can also check your dictionary to see if it contains the specific definition you need. The first one is done as an example.

1. A *bulletin board* is a board on the wall on which people put messages.
   What is an electronic bulletin board? _a system of sending and receiving_
   messages using a computer network

2. To *meet* means to "come together by chance or arrangement." How do
   computer users "meet" in nontraditional ways? _____
   _____

3. *Net* is a shortened form of *network,* a large system of lines, wires, etc. that
   cross or meet one another. If you use an electronic bulletin board, how can
   you make a "net friend?" _____
   _____

4. *Mail* refers to the postal system of sending and receiving letters. What is e-mail? _____

_____

5. A *server* is a person or thing that collects and gives out food. Some computers are <u>servers</u> too. What do they do? _____

_____

6. *Chips* are small pieces of material. What are <u>computer chips</u>?

_____

7. A *program* is a plan of what someone intends to do. When people <u>program</u> a computer, an appliance, or another piece of equipment, what do they do to it? _____

_____

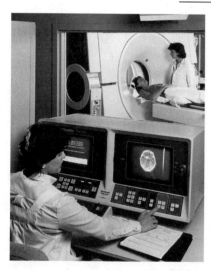

8. To *sense* means to "get a feeling about." Medical technicians can attach <u>sensors</u> to a patient's body. What do these devices do? _____

9. To *slice through* means to "cut into flat pieces." How does photographic equipment such as CAT and DSA <u>slice through</u> body organs? _____

_____

10. People *interact* when they have an effect on one another. What do television, telephones, and computers do in <u>interactive</u> media? _____

_____

Recognizing Reading Structure

 Circle the number of the main idea of the reading.

1. Although there are controversial issues, modern science and technology continue to influence every area of life.

2. Radiation offers both benefits and disadvantages to human beings and the environment.

3. To have a good social life, everyone can make new friends with the help of electronic bulletin boards.

4. Computer technology such as e-mail improves people's communication skills.

 **exercise 4** Here is one way to organize the information in the reading selection. To complete the outline, write words and phrases for topics and subtopics in the blanks. Look back at the reading if necessary. (The letter in parentheses refers to the paragraph that contains the information.)

EVERYDAY USES OF TECHNOLOGY

    I. Social lives through electronic bulletin boards (B)

        A. Locations of computers

            1. _____

            2. Public places

        B. Advantages

            1. Can meet people you might never meet in traditional ways

            2. _____

    II. Communication through e-mail (C)

        A. How it works

            1. _____

            2. _____

        B. Advantage: _____

    III. Computerized equipment in homes (D)

        A. _____

        B. Entertainment equipment

        C. _____

    IV. _____ (E)

        A. _____

            1. Sensors attached to patient's body gather information

            2. Information sent to hospital to prepare for arrival

        B. _____

            1. X-rays, CAT scans, and DSA scans

            2. Other methods

                a. Sonography (sound)

                b. _____

                c. _____

                d. _____

V. _____ (F)

    A. Possible effects of interactive media

        1. Control minds?

        2. _____

        3. _____

    B. _____

    C. Can high-tech medical treatments improve health and happiness?

Understanding Details

Here are some common abbreviations that give clues to the meanings of
details in reading selections.

  i.e. = _id est_ in Latin = that is (in other words)
e.g. = _exempli gratia_ in Latin = for example
etc. = _etcetera_ = and so on (and the rest)

To answer these questions about the details in the reading selection, find the information after or before abbreviations.

    1. What are some aspects of everyday life that technology influences?

    _____

    2. What are some public places with computer terminals? _____

    _____

    3. In computer communication, what is a "server?" _____

    _____

    4. If they are computerized, what kinds of household appliances and

    entertainment equipment might people program? _____

    _____

    5. How are sensors used for medical purposes? _____

    _____

    6. What is an example of a patient in an emergency situation? _____

    7. What are "interactive media?" _____

    8. What is an example of a genetically changed food? _____

    9.   What are some high-tech medical treatments?_____

    _____

 **exercise 6**   Now turn back to the Preparing to Read section on page 220 and answer the questions.

Discussing the Reading

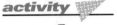 **activity**

In small groups, talk about your answers to the following questions.

1. Do you use or have you ever used an electronic bulletin board or e-mail? If so, explain how they work.

2. What electronic or computerized equipment or appliances do you have in your home? How do you use them?

3. Have you ever been in an ambulance or a hospital during an emergency? If so, what do you remember about medical technology?

4. What are your opinions about the following controversial issues?
   a. Should medical scientists change gene structure to create "more perfect" human beings?
   b. Do you think that computers and interactive media benefit or hurt family life and personal relationships?
   c. Should scientists continue to genetically "improve" foods in the laboratory?
   d. What is the effect of high-tech medical treatments on the health and happiness of people in general?

PART two
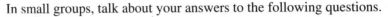

Controversial Issues in Technology

Before You Read
Glancing at Vocabulary

Here are some vocabulary items from the next reading selection. You can learn them now or come back to them later.

NOUNS		VERBS	ADJECTIVES	PHRASES
permission	performance	sue	tiny	invasion of privacy
protection	stress	monitor	electromagnetic	secret password
warrant	interference	invade		electronic surveillance
case	antenna			laser sensor
detection	wings			genetically engineered
receptionist	biotechnology			
speed				

After You Read

Skimming for Main Ideas

exercise 1

Read the following four paragraphs quickly. Then put each of the following titles on the correct line.

Invasion of Privacy Through Electronic Surveillance
Electronic Mysteries in the Sky
Attack of the Killer Tomatoes
Who Can Open the e-Mailbox?

Controversial Issues in Technology

A _____

*L*etters and phone conversations are private. It is against the law to open someone's mail without permission or to secretly listen in on someone's telephone exchange. Furthermore, the U.S. Electronic Communications Privacy Act of 1986 gave the same privacy protections to people who use e-mail. For instance, without a warrant it is illegal for the police to read the messages that a person has received or sent on a computer. Nevertheless, in several cases employees have complained about invasion of privacy on the part of co-workers or their employer. The law is not completely clear on this issue: First of all, each person has a secret password for his or her e-mail, but the company also keeps a complete list of these words. Second, an employer can say, "The company owns everything you have written during worktime because you are using our computer system. Therefore, as things stand right now, it is probably a good idea for computer workers to be careful about the messages they send; an e-mail system may not be the best place for personal thoughts or love letters.

B _____

*E*lectronic surveillance, i.e., a close watch over someone, is the cause of wide disagreement—depending on the purpose of the surveillance. High-tech surveillance systems can be very useful in solving crime cases, in finding missing children, in looking for accident victims, and so on. However, detection devices such as tiny microphones, laser sensors, video cameras, etc., also make electronic surveillance possible in the workplace. In one case, a receptionist with a perfect fourteen-year employment record lost her job because of information collected by the company's computer system. The new monitoring system, which checked on workers' speed and performance, recorded that she was spending about nine minutes "too long" with each visitor or caller. The receptionist, who said she was helping company sales by being friendly to customers, sued her employer in a court of law. She complained that electronic surveillance at work not only causes unnecessary stress but also invades people's privacy.

C

Since 1990, there have been hundreds of reports of mysterious electronic interference with the communications systems of airplanes. Because important flight information—about directions, plane temperature, wind speed, etc.—has disappeared from pilots' computer screens, they have lost their way. Technicians haven't found certain answers to these mysteries, but some people suspect that the cause may be passengers' use of portable computers, electronic games, CD players, etc., inside the plane. Modern airplanes have so many sensors, chips, and wires that they are like "computers with wings"; electromagnetic radiation from entertainment equipment may send confusing signals to airplane antennas.

D

Through biotechnology, scientists can create new foods in the laboratory. For example, they can change a tomato genetically so the fruit can stay on the plant longer, have more taste, and not get soft quickly. They can put a gene from a vegetable plant into a fruit, or even combine some animal genes with plant genes. But are these new foods safe? And what

should the creators and growers have to tell the government, supermarkets, and consumers? Producers claim that genetically engineered products are not much different from traditionally grown foods; nevertheless, some people want to know exactly how scientists changed the DNA material, how many copies of a new gene are in the food, and what problems might come up. For example, will new DNA structures genetically strengthen the bacteria that cause disease?

 **exercise 2**   Answer the following questions about the paragraphs in the reading selection "Controversial Issues in Technology." Then put together your answers to write the main ideas. Paragraph A is done as an example.

PARAGRAPH A

1. What issue is the paragraph about? the privacy of e-mail

2. Why isn't the law clear on this issue? Companies may keep lists of passwords and "own" what employees write.

3. What is the main idea of the paragraph? Laws about the privacy of e-mail aren't clear because companies may keep lists of passwords and "own" what employees write.

PARAGRAPH B

1. What kind of computer system is the paragraph about?

2. Why might people complain about this kind of system?

3. What is the main idea of the paragraph?

PARAGRAPH C

1. What situation is the paragraph about?

2. How might this situation cause problems?

3. What is the main idea of the paragraph?

PARAGRAPH D

1. What kind of technology is the paragraph about?

2. What are some people worried about?

3. What is the main idea of the paragraph?

Inferring: Figuring Out the Meaning

exercise 3   Write 1 on the lines in front of the ideas that the author clearly stated, 2 before the ideas that the writer simply implied, and 3 before the ideas that are not in the reading selection at all. Look back at the reading if necessary.

1. ____ It's illegal to open letters with someone else's name on them without permission.

2. _____ It may or may not be against the law to read someone's e-mail at work.

3. _____ High-tech surveillance systems can include computers, microphones, laser sensors, video cameras, etc.

4. _____ If you lose your job because of electronic surveillance, you will win your case against your employer.

5. _____ Portable computers, electronic games, CD players, and other electronic equipment may have nothing to do with the mysterious interference in airplane computer systems.

6. _____ There will soon be laws against the use of electronic entertainment equipment inside airplanes.

7. _____ Biochemistry will continue to improve the taste and quality of our food.

8. _____ No one knows the effects of genetically engineered food products on people's health.

Learning to Summarize

exercise 4   Work in groups of four. Each student chooses a different paragraph from the reading selection "Controversial Issues in Technology." Summarize the information in your paragraph, beginning with the main idea. Then take turns sharing your summary with your group.

Discussing the Reading

activity   In small groups, talk about your answers to the following questions.

1. In what ways might electronic equipment and surveillance devices lead to invasion of privacy? Who should have the right to use this equipment? In what kinds of situations? Should there be limits on its use?

2. Do you usually feel safe when you take a plane? Do you use or approve of the use of electronic entertainment devices in a plane? Why or why not?

3. Should scientists try to improve the taste of food through genetic engineering? Should they make food last longer? Why or why not?

PART three
Building Vocabulary

Word Usage

As you know, the same word can be more than one part of speech and can have many different meanings. Some of these meanings may be similar, but others may be very much different from one another. Whether you *guess* the meaning of a new vocabulary item or look it up in a dictionary, it is important to choose the appropriate meaning for *that specific context.* If you don't understand the meaning of a word or a phrase correctly, you may not understand the meaning of the sentence or paragraph.

exercise 1

To match each underlined word with its meaning in the sentence, circle the letter of the appropriate definition (N = noun; V = verb; A = adjective or adverb). Which words from the sentence led you to your decision? Circle them. The first one is done as an example.

1. The news media often present controversial issues in science and technology.
   a. N: something printed in a series, such as a magazine.
   b. N: important points or topics of discussion
   c. V: supplies or provides officially

2. A computer owner has gone out on dates with many of the people she has gotten to know through her electronic bulletin board network.
   a. N: times shown by months, days, and years
   b. N: a kind of small, brown, sweet fruit from hot countries
   c. V: social meetings, usually between men and women

3. CAT and DSA scans are photographs that slice through an organ from many different views.
   a. V: reads quickly with the purpose of finding specific information
   b. N: combinations of images (pictures)
   c. V: reads or marks (poetry) to show the structure

4. Too many checks on an employee's speed and performance may create unnecessary job stress.
   a. N: force or pressure caused by difficulties in life
   b. N: emphasis on one or more syllables in a word
   c. V: give importance to

5. Many people complain that they can't understand the instructions on how to <u>program</u> their VCR.
   a. N: a complete TV show
   b. N: a complete plan of things to do, like a series of courses
   c. V: to give (a computer) a plan of what to do

6. Radio <u>waves</u> may interfere with messages to and from airplane antennas.
   a. N: forms in which some forms of energy, such as sound and light, move
   b. N: movement of water, as in the ocean
   c. N: movements of the hand, usually in greeting

7. Our computer romance didn't <u>last</u>, but our interest in word processing did.
   a. A: after everything else; the opposite of *first*
   b. A: at the time nearest to the present; most recent
   c. V: continue; stay in good condition

8. Geneticists can transfer a gene from an animal to a <u>plant</u>, such as a tomato.
   a. N: a living thing, usually with leaves, that grows in the earth
   b. N: a factory
   c. V: to hide things

 For the definitions that you *didn't* choose in Exercise 1, give examples of the vocabulary items in a context of your own. You can find and copy a phrase or sentence from a dictionary or make up your own. You may want to make a vocabulary chart for the eight words, as in Part Three, Chapter Eight, page 167.

examples: 1a. Have you read any recent <u>issues</u> of *Newsweek* magazine?
1c. The U.S. Postal Service often <u>issues</u> new stamps.

focus on testing

Homophones

Reading comprehension and vocabulary tests often include items that ask you to distinguish between two or more homophones. Homophones are words that sound the same but have different spellings and meanings. The most common question type gives sentences with pairs of homophones in parentheses. Your job is to choose the word that best fits in the sentence.

example: Wearing (genes / jeans) and T-shirts, the scientists did experiments on (genes / jeans) all weekend.

Both words are pronounced the same; therefore, to get the correct answers, you had to know that jeans are a kind of pants and that genes are part of the material in the center of a body cell.

exercise 1   Circle the correct homophone in parentheses.

1. When they begin to use electronic (male / mail), many people learn to (write / right) better.
2. Emergency medical technicians attach (sensors / censors) to a (patient's / patience) body to monitor what is going on in the brain and heart.
3. Do the meals on (plains / planes) consist of food (grown / groan) in traditional (ways / weighs)?
4. My birthday is in a (week / weak). I hope some of my (presence / presents) are electronic devices.
5. For the (forth / fourth) time, let's try to (meet / meat) in the laboratory.

exercise 2   Find the homophones of the following words in the reading selection "Controversial Issues in Technology" on pages 229 and 230. Write them on the lines.

1. nose / _____
2. there / _____
3. won / _____
4. buy / _____

5. two / _____ / _____
6. knew / _____
7. sails / _____
8. threw / _____

exercise 3   What other homophones do you know? Work in small groups and make a chart like the following with five pairs of homophones.

homophone	definition	example (phrase or sentence)
1a. meet	V. to get together	When can we meet to discuss the issue?
1b. meat	N. food from animals	Vegetarians don't eat meat.

PART four

Scanning for Information

Working with Tables

exercise

In the areas of science and technology—even more than in other subject areas—information often appears in list, table, or chart form. Work in small groups. Look at the chart of important scientific inventions and technological advances. Read the questions at the end of the chart. Find the information quickly.

year	invention or advance	inventor or origin
1285	eyeglasses	Alessandra de Spina
1784	bifocal lenses	Benjamin Franklin
1798	mass production	Eli Whitney
1812	canned food	Bryan Doukin
1826	gas stove	James Sharp
1827	microphone	Charles Wheatstone
1846	sewing machine	Elias Howe
1850	refrigerator	James Harrison and Alexander Twining
1857	passenger elevator	Elisha G. Otis
1886	Coca-Cola	John Pemberton
1887	contact lenses	Eugen A. Frick
1890	motion pictures	William Friese Greene

year	invention or advance	inventor or origin
1911	air-conditioning	Willis H. Carrier
1924	frozen food	Clarence Birdseye
1945	artificial kidney	Willem J. Kolff
1958	laser	Charles H. Townes
1960	weather satellite	NASA, United States
1964	home videotape recorder	Sony, Japan
1965	word processor	IBM, United States
1969	jumbo jet plane	Joe Sutherland at Boeing, United States
1972	video game	Noland Bushnel
1973	microcomputer	Trong Truong
1977	space shuttle	NASA, United States
1982	artificial heart	Robert Jarvik
1984	compact-disk player	Sony and Fujitsu Companies
1989	gene transfer	Steven Rosenberg

1. Which dates (years) surprise you? Circle them. Tell why you find them surprising.

2. Which inventions or advances are you familiar with? Circle them. Tell how you think they have changed since their beginning.

3. Which inventors have your heard of? Circle them. Tell the class what you know about them.

4. Which inventions or advances do you think are the most important to the world today? (Circle no more than ten.) Tell the reasons for your decision.

Going Beyond the Text

Bring to class some charts, tables, or graphs on scientific and technological subjects (e.g., numerical tables of measures or temperature, a chemical-elements chart, illustrations of how machines work, etc.). Perhaps you can make a transparency of the chart or illustration for an overhead projector. Explain your material to the class by answering these questions.

1. What is the topic of the chart or illustration? What does it show?
2. Why is it important?
3. Explain the important numbers, machine parts, and steps in the process.

PART five
Personal Story

The Trouble with Technology

The following story tells about the writer's experience with high-tech equipment.

 **exercise**

Follow these steps for the story:

1. Read it quickly and tell the main idea.

2. Answer your instructor's questions about the story, or ask and answer questions of your own.

3. Tell your own opinions of the ideas in the story. For example, tell how you think the story will end.

4. Tell or write about your own experiences with science and technology.

I'm always reading ads for new products, such as computer parts and software, wireless speakers and headphones for sound systems, compact camcorders, color laser copiers, electronic book players, and many others. Like thousands of other people, I'm interested in modern technological equipment and devices. Of course, I don't always understand how a product works, and I certainly don't know all the technological words in the ad, but somehow I'm fascinated, and I want that machine! Occasionally, I buy it. As soon as I bring my new "toy" home or to my office, I have trouble reading the long, complex manual or even the short booklet—the language just isn't clear or simple enough for me. When my children help, however, I can usually figure out how to set up the new equipment or device. But then something happens to cause a mechanical or electronic problem. Because I don't know how to fix it myself, I call the store where I bought it for advice. If the salespeople can't help, I bring the product to a repair shop. However, even after paying for new parts and a repairperson's time, I still can't get the product to work the same way it used to. Eventually, I lose interest in the machine or device—or in *any* technological products at all. I start to *read* again—books and newspapers and magazines. Soon I see ads for new technological products that fascinate me, so. . . .

WHAT DO YOU THINK?

All areas of life, including technology, can include humor. Here are some funny stories related to modern machines. For each story, discuss your answers to these questions:

1. What is the point (the joke) of the story?
2. Does the story seem funny to you? Why or why not?
3. Does the story remind you of any real experiences in your life? Explain.

1   Like many modern businesses, the bank where I work has a "voice mail" answering-machine system. When callers dial our number, they receive a long series of messages, such as:

> If you're calling from a touch-tone phone, please press 1.
> If you want to hear messages in English, please press 2.
> If you want to check the balance in your account, please press 3.
> If you are applying for a loan, please press 4.

One customer had to go through the whole series of messages, then wait quite a while longer before a human being finally answered the phone.

> "May I have your account number?" asked the bank representative.
> "If you want my account number," the customer replied, "please press 1."

2   In anatomy class, the instructor was giving a lecture about the human nervous system. Before explaining the concept of *neurotransmission* (the process through which nerve cells send electrochemical signals), the instructor first asked the class, "Can anyone tell us how cells communicate with each other?"
   After some silence, a voice asked, "With cellular phones?"

You, the Consumer

in this chapter

Are you a smart consumer? The first reading selection talks about the influence that advertising has on what we buy and don't buy. The second selection gives advice on how to shop intelligently. In the final reading, you will find out about an interesting shopping experience.

Advertising: The Selling of a Product

Before You Read

Getting Started

Look at the picture and talk about it.

1. Where is the person? What is he trying to do?
2. Why is he confused?
3. What kind of product is he looking at?
4. Do you think these products are similar to one another or different from one another?

Preparing to Read

Think about the answers to the following questions. The reading selection will answer them.

1. What influences us when we decide to buy one product instead of another?
2. What kind of information do we get from advertising?
3. What methods do advertisers use to sell products?
4. Who is not affected by advertising?

Glancing at Vocabulary

Here are some vocabulary items from the first reading selection. You can learn them now or come back to them later.

NOUNS	VERBS	ADJECTIVES	PHRASES
consumer	pick	complete	instead of
consumerism	admit	stupid	on the market
advertiser	realize		self-image
advertising			get . . . to
package			

Read the following selection quickly. Then do the exercises after the reading.

Advertising: The Selling of a Product

A consumer walks into a store. He stands in front of hundreds of boxes of laundry detergent. He chooses one brand, pays for it, and leaves. Why does he pick that specific kind of soap? Is it truly better than the others? Probably not. These days, many products are nearly identical to one another in quality and price. If products are almost the same, what makes consumers buy one brand instead of another? Although we might not like to admit it, commercials on television and advertisements in magazines probably influence us much more than we think they do.

Advertising informs consumers about new products available on the market. It gives us information about everything from shampoo to toothpaste to computers and cars. But there is one serious problem with this. The "information" is actually very often *mis*information. It tells us the products' benefits but hides their disadvantages. Advertising not only leads us to buy things that we don't need and can't afford, but it also confuses our sense of reality. "Zoom toothpaste prevents cavities and gives you white teeth!" the advertisement tells us. But it doesn't tell us the complete truth: that a healthy diet and a good toothbrush will have the same effect.

Advertisers use many methods to get us to buy their products. One of their most successful methods is to make us feel dissatisfied with ourselves and our imperfect lives. Advertisements show us who we aren't and what we don't have. Our teeth aren't white enough. Our hair isn't shiny enough. Our clothes aren't clean enough. Advertisements make us afraid that people won't like us if we don't use the advertised products. "Why don't I have any dates?" an attractive young woman sadly asks in a commercial. "Here," replies her roommate, "try Zoom toothpaste!" Of course she tries it, and immediately the whole football team falls in love with her. "That's a stupid commercial," we might say. But we still buy Zoom toothpaste out of fear of being unpopular and having no friends.

If fear is the negative motive for buying a product, then wanting a good self-image is the positive reason for choosing it. Each of us has a mental picture of the kind of person we would like to be. For example, a modern young woman might like to think that she looks like a beautiful movie star. A middle-aged man might want to see himself as a strong, attractive athlete. Advertisers know this. They write specific ads to make certain groups of people choose their product. Two people may choose different brands of toothpaste with the identical price, amount, and quality; each person believes that he or she is expressing his personality by choosing that brand.

E   Advertisers get psychologists to study the way consumers think and their reasons for choosing one brand instead of another. These experts tell advertisers about the motives of fear and self-image. They also inform them about recent studies with colors and words. Psychologists have found that certain colors on the package of an attractive product will cause people to reach out and take that package instead of buying an identical product with different colors. Also, certain words attract our attention. For example, the words "new," "improved," "natural," and "giant size" are very popular and seem to draw our eyes and hands toward the package.

F   Many people believe that advertising does not affect them. They feel that they have freedom of choice, and they like to think they make wise choices. Unfortunately, they probably don't realize the powerful effect of advertising. They may not clearly understand that advertisers spend billions of dollars each year in aggressive competition for our money, and they are extremely successful. Do you believe that ads don't influence your choice of products? Just look at the brands in your kitchen and bathroom.

After You Read

Getting the Main Ideas

 Write T (true), F (false), or I (impossible to know from the reading) on the lines.

1. _____ Advertising influences us to buy one kind of product instead of another.

2. _____ Advertisements always provide us with important information about products.

3. _____ Wanting a good self-image is a powerful reason for choosing products.

4. _____ If you use Zoom toothpaste, there will be no more problems in your life.

5. _____ The "Psychology of Selling" is an important course in many business colleges.

Guessing Meaning from Context

 **exercise 2**   Circle the words that give clues to the meaning of the underlined word. Then write a definition of each word on the line. Check your answers in a dictionary.

1. A consumer chooses one brand of <u>detergent</u>, pays for it, and leaves. Why does he pick that specific kind of soap?_____

_____

2. These days, many products are nearly <u>identical</u> to one another in quality and price. If they are almost the same, what makes us buy one brand instead of another?_____

3. Advertising <u>informs</u> us about new products available on the market, but it tells us only of their benefits._____

4. Advertising gives us information about products, but there is a problem: The "information" is actually very often <u>misinformation</u>._____

_____

5. "Zoom toothpaste prevents <u>cavities</u> and gives you white teeth!" the advertisement tells us. _____

6. If fear is the negative <u>motive</u> for buying a product, then wanting a good self-image is the positive reason for choosing it._____

_____

7. Wanting a good <u>self-image</u> is the positive reason for choosing some products. Each of us has a mental picture of the kind of person we would like to be. _____

8. Advertisers regularly get <u>psychologists</u> to study the way consumers think and their motives for choosing one brand instead of another.

_____

9. Certain words attract our attention. For example, the words "new" and "improved" are very popular and seem to draw our eyes and hands toward an <u>attractive</u> package._____

10. Many people believe that advertising does not <u>affect</u> them. Do you believe that ads influence your choice of products?_____

_____

Recognizing Reading Structure

exercise 3 On the lines, write the main idea of the reading.

_____

_____

exercise 4 Outline the selection by writing the main ideas on the appropriate lines. The words in parentheses are the main topics—cues to help you; the letters in parentheses at the ends of the lines refer to the lettered paragraphs in the reading.

    I. (Introduction) _____ (A)

   II. (Misinformation in advertising) _____

     _____ (B)

       A. (Benefits of products) _____

       B. (Disadvantages) _____

       C. (Reality) _____

  III. (Methods of advertisers) _____

     _____

       A. (Fear) _____ (C)

       B. (Self-image) _____ (D)

       C. (Colors and words) _____ (E)

  IV. (Conclusion) _____ (F)

Understanding Details

> Sometimes a writer exaggerates (makes something seem more than it really is) or uses humor to make a point. The reader knows that the information is not exactly true but understands the author's reason for exaggerating.
>
> *example:* "Zoom toothpaste prevents cavities and gives you white teeth!" (There is no toothpaste called Zoom; the author intends, humorously, for the name to suggest speed, modernity, and other qualities of "wonderful" products.)

exercise 5 Circle the letter that indicates the "real meaning" of each of the following sentences.

1. This product makes clothes whiter than white!
   a. This product is only for clothes that are white.
   b. This product will clean clothes well.
   c. This product will change the color of clothes.

2. Our teeth aren't white enough. Our hair isn't shiny enough. Our clothes aren't clean enough.
   a. We should wash our clothes with toothpaste and shampoo.
   b. To improve ourselves, we should immediately buy the products in the commercials.
   c. We should go to a psychologist to talk about our problems.

3. In the commercial, she tries Zoom toothpaste and immediately the whole football team falls in love with her.
   a. According to commercials, people will like you better if you use their products.
   b. Zoom toothpaste is the best in the world.
   c. Football players often fall in love with actresses in commercials.

4. A modern young woman might like to think that she looks like a beautiful movie star.
   a. A modern young woman wants to be as attractive as possible.
   b. Every modern young woman wants to act in movies.
   c. Most modern women think that they are beautiful.

5. A middle-aged man might want to see himself as a strong, attractive athlete.
   a. All middle-aged men are in good physical health.
   b. Older men should all get exercise in the gym.
   c. Men usually want to look as attractive as possible.

exercise 6 Circle the letters of *all* the correct answers for each of the following blanks.

1. Advertising _____ .
   a. informs us about some products
   b. doesn't influence us very much
   c. misinforms us
   d. doesn't always tell us everything about a product

2. A person often buys a product because _____ .
   a. he or she is dissatisfied with himself or herself
   b. of a need for a good self-image
   c. of the colors on the package
   d. of certain words on the package

3. Advertisers _____ to make us buy products.
   a. offer very low prices
   b. get information from psychologists
   c. spend a lot of money
   d. need to use better detergent and shampoo

4. Psychologists tell advertisers _____ .
   a. which brands of toothpaste to produce
   b. to stop influencing shoppers
   c. about people's motives for buying
   d. how much money to spend on television commercials

5. The words _____ on products are very popular and seem to attract our attention.
   a. "really cheap"
   b. "giant size"
   c. "new and improved"
   d. "good enough"

exercise 7 Now turn back to the Preparing to Read section on page 242 and answer the questions.

Discussing the Reading

In small groups, talk about your answers to the following questions.

1. What kinds of advertising attracts your attention? Do you sometimes buy the products in the ads or commercials?
2. How are American and Canadian advertisements and commercials different from those in your country? How are they similar?
3. Are there any rules or laws about advertising in your country?
4. What image would you like to have for yourself? Would you like to be similar to any people you see in television commercials or magazine ads?
5. What famous brands of products do you have in your home now? Why did you buy them?

PART two
Smart Shopping

Before You Read

Glancing at Vocabulary

Here are some vocabulary items from the next reading selection. You can learn them now or come back to them later.

NOUN	VERB	ADJECTIVES	PHRASES
manufacturer	compare	generic	piece of advice
		discount	grocery store
		plain	small print
			on sale
			name brands
			dressing room

Skimming for Main Ideas

 Read each of the following four paragraphs quickly. Then write the main idea of each paragraph on the line.

Smart Shopping

ADVICE FOR CONSUMERS

A   **M**ost mothers have a good piece of advice: Never go into a supermarket hungry! If you go shopping for food before lunchtime, you'll probably buy more than you plan to. Unfortunately, however, just this simple advice isn't enough for consumers these days. Modern shoppers need an education in how—and how not—to buy things at the grocery store. First, you should check out the weekly newspaper ads. Find out the items that are on sale and decide if you really need those things. In other words, don't buy anything just because it's cheaper than usual. Next, in the market, carefully read the information on the package, and don't let words like "New and Improved" or "All Natural" on the front of a package influence you. Instead, read the list of ingredients on the back. Third, compare prices; that is, you should examine the prices both of different brands and different sizes of the same brand.

The main idea: _____

_____

GENERIC ITEMS AND BRAND NAMES

B

Another suggestion for consumers is to buy generic items instead of famous brands. Generic items in supermarkets come in plain packages. These products are cheaper because manufacturers don't spend much money on packaging or advertising. The quality, however, is usually identical to the quality of well-known name brands. In the same way, when buying clothes, you can often find high quality and low prices in brands that are not famous. Shopping in discount clothing stores can also help you save a lot of money. Although these stores aren't very attractive, and they usually do not have individual dressing rooms, the prices are low, and you can often find the same famous brands that you find in high-priced department stores.

The main idea: _____

_____

INTELLIGENT CONSUMERISM

C

Wise consumers read magazine advertisements and watch TV commercials, but they do this with one advantage: knowledge of the psychology behind the ads. In other words, well-informed consumers watch for information and check for misinformation. They ask themselves questions: Is the advertiser hiding something in small print at the bottom of the page? Is there any real information in the commercial, or is the advertiser simply showing an attractive image? Is this product more expensive than it should be because it has a famous name? With the answers to these questions, consumers can make a wise choice.

The main idea: _____

_____

CONSUMER PROTECTION LAWS

D

To protect consumers, there are many laws (usually state laws) about advertising. For instance, if a store advertises a special product at a certain price, the store must have a reasonable number of items to sell so that it doesn't run out of them right away. A sale ad may mention a limit on quantity, but if it doesn't, you have the right to buy as many of the items as you want. The product should not look much different from the picture in the ad. Also, an advertiser must tell you if a product is used or defective. In other words, false and misleading advertising is against the law.

The main idea: _____

_____

After You Read
Viewpoint

 Complete the following sentence.

The author of the reading selection implies her point of view. Her opinion of advertising is that _____

_____

_____

_____

Inferring: Figuring Out the Meaning

 Write 1 on the lines in front of the ideas that the author clearly stated, 2 before the ideas that the writer simply implied, and 3 before the ideas that are not in the reading selection at all. Look back at the selection if necessary.

1. _____ People who shop for groceries when they are hungry usually buy more than people who shop after dinner.

2. _____ Items on sale are cheaper than usual.

3. _____ It's a good idea to read the ingredients on the back of a package.

4. _____ Sometimes it's better to buy one size of a product than another.

5. _____ Generic items never say "New and Improved!" or "All Natural!"

6. _____ Generic products are usually cheaper than famous brands.

7. _____ To save money, you should buy clothes in discount stores rather than in expensive department stores.

8. _____ An intelligent shopper knows something about the psychology of selling.

9. _____ It is illegal to try to mislead consumers through false advertising.

10. _____ If a store has too few advertised items, limits quantity, or doesn't tell buyers that the products are used or defective, consumers may sue.

Learning to Summarize

> You can summarize better if you are aware of the purpose of a reading selection. For instance, if the main purpose is to give advice—as in the reading selection "Smart Shopping"—a good summary might consist of a list of the pieces of advice.

exercise 3

The four paragraphs in the reading selection "Smart Shopping" answer the question "How can a consumer be a smart shopper?" Work in groups of four. Each student chooses a different paragraph from the reading. List (in paragraph or list form) all the advice in your paragraph. Then take turns sharing your list with your group. Finally, combine your lists to make one summary.

Discussing the Reading

activity

In small groups, talk about your answers to the following questions.

1. Has your mother ever given you any advice about shopping? If so, what was the advice?

2. Do you buy generic items? Why or why not?

3. Are consumer-protection laws in the United States and Canada different from such laws in your country? If so, how?

4. How is shopping in the United States and Canada different from shopping in your country?

5. What advice can you give a visitor who wants to go shopping in your country?

PART three
Building Vocabulary

Compound Adjectives

The Focus on Testing section in Chapter Three, page 50, discussed compound nouns. In addition to nouns, compound words can also be adjectives. Most compound adjectives consist of an adjective—often ending in *-ed* or *-ing*—plus a noun, or an adverb plus an adjective.

examples: Adjective + Noun
low + cost = low-cost (low-cost housing)

Adverb + Adjective
well + known = well-known (a well-known brand name)

Most compound adjectives are joined by a hyphen when they come before a noun; when they follow the noun, they are often written as two words, without a hyphen.

examples: It is difficult to find low-cost housing in this area.
That brand name is very well known.

exercise 1   Complete the sentences with the following compound adjectives.

good-looking	high-fiber	well-known
name-brand	English-speaking	sweet-tasting
well-informed	long-lived	

1. I buy _____ clothes in discount stores because I can't afford them in expensive department stores.

2. _____ shoppers know about the prices and the quality of products.

3. In television commercials, _____ people often buy products out of fear of being unpopular.

4. Do the _____ people of healthful mountainous areas need to buy medicines and chemicals to improve their lives?

5. Some consumers prefer _____ toothpaste, so they buy brands that taste like candy.

6. I saw a _____ movie star in the department store the other day.

7. Advertisements for _____ cereals might attract people interested in eating healthier food.

8. Advertising on most TV channels in the United States is for _____ consumers, but some channels have ads for viewers who speak other languages.

exercise 2   Write a compound adjective to complete each of the following definitions. The first two are done as examples. When you make a compound adjective from a compound noun, drop the -s from the noun.

1. A marriage that has lasted thirty years is a ___thirty-year___ marriage.

2. A brand name that is famous around the world is _____ .

3. A house with two bedrooms is a _____ house.

4. Most fruits and vegetables are free of fat, so they are considered _____ foods.

5. Places that serve fast food are called _____ restaurants.

6. The quality of items in discount stores is often very high; in other words, many discount stores sell _____ items.

7. The section in a supermarket where you can buy frozen food is called the
   _____ section.

8. A marathon is a running race that goes for approximately 26 miles; in other
   words, a marathon is a _____ run.

focus on testing

Idiomatic Expressions

Idiomatic expressions—phrases that mean something different from the separate words—usually appear on reading and vocabulary tests. Often, these are phrasal verbs. The most common question type is multiple-choice: You read sentences with an underlined idiom, and you have to choose the answer that is closest in meaning to the expression or phrase.

example: Before you go food shopping, check out the weekly newspaper ads.

   a. cut out   **c.** remember
   b. pay for   **d.** examine

Since all four choices make a correct sentence, you have to know the meaning of check out in order to get the correct answer.

exercise   Each sentence in 1 to 4 has an underlined phrasal verb that is an idiomatic expression. Below each sentence are four choices. Choose the one expression or phrase that is closest in meaning to the underlined expression. Circle the letter of the correct answer.

1. When you go shopping, find out the items that are on sale.
   a. locate   **c.** learn
   b. choose   **d.** remember

2. The store manager got rid of all the dishonest employees.
   a. knew about   **c.** spoke to
   b. fired   **d.** laughed at

3. A lot of people came to buy the product we advertised, so we ran out.
   a. had no more   **c.** moved quickly
   b. were tired   **d.** stopped working

4. They had to call off the sale because the items didn't arrive on time.
   a. telephone people about   **c.** cancel
   b. visit   **d.** speak loudly about

PART four

Scanning for Information

Magazine Ads

exercise

As you have seen from this chapter, it is important for a consumer to carefully examine products. It is also important to understand the psychology of advertising. Look at the following ads and answer the questions about them on page 256.

1.

2.

3.

4.

1. What product is advertised in the four ads?_____

2. What kind of person do you see in ad 1?_____

   How is he dressed? _____

   What might his profession be? _____

3. What kind of person do you see in ad 2?_____

   How is she dressed? _____

   What might her profession be? _____

   What does her body language tell you? _____

4. Where are the people in ad 3? _____

   How are they dressed?_____

   In your opinion, what kind of people might they be? _____

   _____

5. Where is the man in ad 4? _____

   How is he dressed? _____

   What words in this ad might attract some people? _____

   _____

6. What is the self-image of a person who might be attracted to:

   ad 1? _____

   ad 2? _____

   ad 3? _____

   ad 4? _____

7. What does ad 3 lead the reader to think about the product?

   _____

   What misinformation can you find in ads 3 and 4? _____

   _____

Going Beyond the Text

exercise

In small groups, look through magazines for advertisements about another kind of product. List the brand names. List the words that are used in several or all the ads. Discuss them. What is their purpose? What image might they express? What kind of consumers do the ads want to attract? Then list the words that are in only one ad. How does this ad differ from other ads? Finally, listen to TV commercials. Which words are the same as in magazine ads? Which are different? Why?

PART **five**
Personal Stories

Shopping

The following story tells about a shopping experience from the author's child-hood.

exercise ▸▸▸

Follow these steps for the story:

1. Read it quickly and tell the main idea.
2. Answer your instructor's questions about the story, or ask and answer questions of your own.
3. Tell your own opinions of the ideas in the story.

Big Business

Back in my country, when I was a child, I used to go to "market day" with my mother. One day each week, farmers used to bring their fruit and vegetables into the city. They closed one street to all cars, and the farmers set up tables for their produce. This outdoor market was a great place to shop. Everything was fresher than produce in grocery stores because the farmers brought it in immediately after the harvest. My mother and I always got there early in the morning to get the freshest produce.

The outdoor market was a wonderful adventure for a small child. It was like a festival—full of colors and sounds. There were red tomatoes, yellow lemons, green lettuce, peppers, grapes, onions. The farmers did their own advertising. They all shouted loudly for customers to buy their produce. "Come and buy my beautiful oranges! They're juicy and delicious and full of vitamins to make your children healthy and strong!"

Chapter Twelve • You, the Consumer

257

Everyone used to argue with the farmers over the price of their produce. It was like a wonderful drama in a theater; the buyers and sellers were the "actors" in this drama. My mother was an expert at this. First, she picked the freshest, most attractive tomatoes, for example. Then she asked the price. The seller told her.

"What?" she said. She looked very surprised. "So expensive?"

The seller looked terribly hurt. "My dear lady!" he replied. "I am a poor, honest farmer. These are the cheapest tomatoes on the market!"

They always argued for several minutes before agreeing on a price. My mother took her tomatoes and left. Both buyer and seller were satisfied. The drama was over.

WHAT DO YOU THINK?

All areas of life can include humor. Here are some funny stories related to shopping and consumerism. Discuss your answers to these questions:

1. What is the point of each story?
2. Does the story seem funny to you? Why or why not?
3. Does the story remind you of any real experiences in your life? Explain.

1   One evening, we were interrupted by sales calls several times during dinner. Telephone solicitors were trying to do marketing surveys, provide us with more insurance, sell us long-lasting light bulbs, and so on. Around dessert time, the phone rang again.

Our twenty-year-old son Brian answered this time. By his comments, we assumed he was talking to his friend Jim, who likes to play jokes on people. He kept saying things like, "Oh, come on, Jim. I know it's you. You've played this joke before."

When he hung up after a few minutes, we asked, innocently, "That was Jim?"

"No, it was another telephone solicitor," said Brian, smiling. "I don't think he'll call again."

2   The parts manager of a small electronics company ordered Part Number 966 from the factory. But when it arrived, he noticed that the factory had sent Part Number 996 instead.

The manager needed the part right away, so he was upset about the mistake. He sent the box back to the factory with an angry letter. A week later, however, he received the same box back, with a short note. It said, "Turn the box over."